THE
MUSLIM
ENTREPRENEUR

10 SUCCESS PRINCIPLES

FROM THE GREATEST

MUSLIM ENTREPRENEURS

THE
MUSLIM
ENTREPRENEUR

10 SUCCESS PRINCIPLES

FROM THE GREATEST

MUSLIM ENTREPRENEURS

Oumar Soule

Bilal Success

Published by Bilal Success, Canada
First published in 2015. This is a revised edition with a new foreword.
Design and composition by Arub Saqib.
Book manufacturer: Lightning Source

Oumar Soule.
Ten Success Principles from the Greatest Muslim Entrepreneurs revised edition.

To my parents Souleymane and Aminata,

my wife Arub,

and my siblings,

who encouraged me

to finish this book.

CONTENTS

FOREWORD

by Dr. Hatim Zaghloul

I was contacted a few years ago by Oumar. He asked to interview me for a new book he was authoring about successful Muslim entrepreneurs. I realized that this was a wonderful and needed undertaking. I told him "you're doing the right thing."

We rarely hear about the great successes of modern Muslims in business. I was very impressed after reading the book. The stories of successful Muslim entrepreneurs are very inspiring and uplifting.

We can be happy and content with what Allah has blessed us with but that should not stop us from working tirelessly on improving our condition.

As the co-inventor of Wi-Fi and LTE technologies and the founder of several successful technology companies, I know the importance of having the right information. I always say "a smart person learns from his own mistakes and past successes. But a wise person learns from the mistakes and successes of others."

By reading this book, you will learn about:

The difference between the Muslim Entrepreneur and everyone else.
Why should you consider joining the ranks of the Muslim Entrepreneurs?
What are the thought processes and the actions required to be successful?
What are some of the challenges facing Muslim entrepreneurs?

Oumar's book provides us with those answers. Whenever possible, this book has avoided theories and feel-good advice. Instead, Oumar gives us practical advice from 40 of some of the greatest Muslim Entrepreneurs of the last two decades.

By studying our business practices, scrutinizing our habits and condensing them into this easy to follow manual you hold in your hands, Oumar has developed a framework from which I hope great things will happen.

I think that this book could show you the path to great wealth as a Muslim Entrepreneur. It contains ten secrets of success that have been tested and verified. I urge you to read it and apply it.

Wishing you the greatest success.

Hatim Zaghloul
Wi-Fi inventor,
Founder of Inovatian Inc , WiLan Inc.

INTRODUCTION

Do you want to be a wealthy Muslim?

Would you like to know who the successful Muslims are and what are they doing?

If so, you are at the right place.

I am going to introduce to you some of the world's most brilliant Muslim Entrepreneurs. They have opened up and shared their secrets.

The world of business and success is tough and very competitive. Some other authors have written extensively on the subject of success. They also have covered the biographies of successful entrepreneurs.

However, that information is only partially relevant to a Muslim audience since a big part of success is dependent on one's beliefs and spiritual values. This is the first book that deals exclusively with Muslim Entrepreneurs.

What are they doing to win big in today's competitive environment?

I had the privilege to interview 40 of them and this book is the result.

This information is purely derived from the teachings of Muslim Entrepreneurs that are achieving an unusual level of success in terms of income, impact and originality. These entrepreneurs are from different parts of the World – from the Indian subcontinent to the Middle East to Africa, Europe and North America.

You are in for a ride! Buckle your seat belt! To the Author's knowledge, this is the first time such a book has been released in the last few centuries.

So, if you're wondering; how can I make a lot of money as a Muslim?

How can I gain an advantage over the rest?

What can I do with my money?

What challenges can I expect along the way?

What skills do I need to succeed in today's marketplace?

Then know that these are exactly the questions "The Muslim Entrepreneur" answers. And much more!

I will see you on the other side inshaAllah.

PRINCIPLE I

THE MUSLIM ADVANTAGE

1

ISLAM AND WEALTH

ISLAM WANTS YOU WEALTHY

The Muslim Entrepreneur does his best while relying on Allah SWT. We as human beings are dependant on God as our Provider. We are all dependent on rain and land for food, clothes and shelter after all; every single one of us - since Adam (AS)! So, all of us are invited to seek sustenance but also ask our Creator.

That is why some of the prophets were actually extremely wealthy. They asked Allah, their Provider. One story that comes to mind is Sulaiman (AS). He was the son of king Dawud. He was also a messenger of Allah. After thanking Allah for the wealth he already had been blessed with, he asked to be given more than anybody in the whole universe. That is ambition right there! He was known to own a kingdom not just on earth but also on the air, the sea and even the invisible kingdom of the Jinns.

The prophets are known to be the best of humans and the best examples to follow. It should be clear that those examples are given in the Qur'an so that we may benefit and even emulate them.When you ask, take into consideration the One you are asking.

He owns everything; so make sure you ask a lot!

God is Infinite and can bless you with infinite wealth. When you go see one of the richest men alive maybe Bill Gates or prince AlWaleed bin Talal, and they offered you a chance to get funding for whatever project you want to work on, how much will you ask for? Would you go to the trouble of getting his time just to ask for a new laptop, or a thousand dollars? Or would you go for a significant project?

Now, consider the fact that Allah created that rich man; owns him and everything he has. So ask more my friend, and watch what happens.

THOSE MUSLIMS LEFT A FORTUNE

The prophet SAW himself was an entrepreneur. This is reflected in all the accounts of his life. You can see how this affects any Muslim individual who is following his teachings (sunnah). When he was about 12 years of age, he went to Syria with his uncle Abu Talib on a caravan. The Meccans used to pool their resources together to venture in trade. They would buy merchandise from Syria and sell them in Arabia. The Syrians would buy Arabian goods from them in exchange.

During his early twenties he became a manager for a wealthy noble woman Khadija Bint Khuwaylid (RA) whom he eventually married.

Islam is unique in that it developed in the most active trading cities of old Arabia. And the Islamic Faith continued to spread through trade. The Silk Road, spanning three continents, is one example of how trade defined Muslim identity.

In my study of Muslim Entrepreneurs, I interviewed a few people from the Muslim trading families of the Silk Road that migrated to Africa.

They brought with them the belief that there is opportunity everywhere you go. Today, some of them are multi-millionaires.

You too can have this attitude. And it is a big advantage for you. There is no contradiction between reaching success in this life and the next thanks to the example of the prophet SAW and his amazing companions.
The majority of the Sahaba that were promised paradise died wealthy.

When Sa'ad ibn Abbi Waqqas (RA) passed away, he left a fortune so big that it took three years to estimate all his wealth and distribute inheritance between wives, children and close relatives. This is an aspect of the lives of the companions that is often neglected.

We also have the example of Uthman Ibn Affan (RA) who was reputed to own half of all the business conducted in Muslim lands at one point. Try to imagine nowadays a multi-millionaire imam or scholar. The good news is that you will have the opportunity to meet some of them as the book progresses.

THEY DID IT RIGHT

The Quran clearly emphasizes trade. One such passage is with the prophet Shuaib (AS), who told his people:

"Give full measure and do not be of those who cause loss. And weigh with an even [i.e. honest] balance. And do not deprive people of their due and do not commit abuse on earth, spreading corruption."

-Al-Quran, Surah Ash-Shu'araa, Ayah 181-183

The prophets were honest and upright. Our prophet (SAW) was known as the trustworthy one – Al Amin. He prospered through honesty.

According to Dr. Miles Davis, an African American Muslim dean of the Shenondoah business school:

"Everybody wants good quality products and services. If the other party knows your reputation for quality and honesty then you are golden."

-Dr. Miles Davis, Business School Dean

On one incident, the prophet (SAW) showcased the epitome of honesty. He was so honest that even those plotting against him left their gold and other valuables in his care.

They were plotting to kill him; yet they did not take their money back. That was because they trusted his service.

He was trustworthy, truthful in speech and action. He was upright.

That is the reason why some traders prosper; because of trust. The stock market would not work without trust. The Internet would not have worked either. Say I want to buy a laptop from a website. I log in to the website that I have to trust. Then I click a button to buy the laptop and the money is taken from my account. I don't have the laptop, yet I already paid. The only reason why I might be comfortable with the situation is if I believe the website owners will honour their word and send me the laptop. Without trust everything is much slower. In an environment with little trust I might want to visit the store in person, get the name of the owner and maybe even get their address. You get the picture. Lack of trust means slow business.

So get the trust factor up if you want to prosper. It takes a lifetime to build this trust and it can be ruined in an instant. We can even go a step further and say that trustworthiness is the biggest part of character.

Once you know that someone is trustworthy you can be sure that they are not hiding anything from you. This is crucial in your business dealings.

At the end of the day, you can never hide from your own self. We can hide from the public but we cannot hide from our own selves. Once we have succeeded as entrepreneurs, it is important to keep being true to ourselves and avoid long-term self-sabotage.

That is when intention plays a major role. Are we getting wealthy just for show or to look good ? Or are we working to help relatives, people and worship Allah SWT?

We will talk more about this point on the chapter of Work Ethics.

THE BEST EXAMPLE

The prophetic character is unique and exceptional. The Messenger Muhammad SAW is viewed by many as the most successful person who ever lived. He grew up as an orphan and lived in poverty during his childhood. Yet, after the prophetic mission, he became the chief of state of a prosperous and peaceful region that went on to become one of the largest empires that ever existed. Many subsequent states were inspired by Islamic principles long after that initial state weakened and disappeared.

Some have argued that there are also many good teachings in Christianity, Judaism, Buddhism and so on. That is true. But how many prophets actually give sound investment advice that you can apply today? I could not find any apart from the prophet Muhammad SAW. The prophet SAW even taught us what to do with your money once you sell your house. And this is a great advantage for the Muslim entrepreneur.

That is why today, in the 21st century, many Muslim leaders in business are following his principles and philosophies.

SOCIAL JUSTICE

Social justice is a key pursuit of the Muslim Entrepreneur. Any society knows that justice brings peace and more prosperity.

The most successful entrepreneurs I met are also the most giving. They truly serve and are always helping people and the communities they live in.

Azim Rizvee is a world-class entrepreneur whom I had the opportunity to talk to. He has made major contributions to the community in which he lives in Ontario, Canada. His city is now one of the fastest growing in the country. He started literally from zero and within two to three years became the number one brokerage firm. Along with some very successful Muslim entrepreneurs and the local community, he is spearheading a project that will help his local hospital get an extra wing. Rizvee and his league of Muslim Entrepreneurs have called it 'The Muslim Legacy Wing'.

It is truly remarkable to see how service to people leads to prosperity.
Now, there are businesses that are completely forbidden by the religion such as gambling, alcohol etc. During the interviewing process, we have done our best to avoid any business that generates a big part of its income through unlawful means.

Apart from those extreme cases, a Muslim Entrepreneur will only prosper long-term if he serves the greatest number of people through goods and services he provides.

You might object that some Muslims got wealthy by cheating or being dishonest. But that is often not the whole truth.

Ask yourself this: "what services do these entrepreneurs provide to people? How many people are being employed because of them?" Then you will realize that all the very successful entrepreneurs follow the principles of Social Justice. If they have long term success, they are implementing this Islamic value.

To ensure total justice, Islam goes a step further by prohibiting interest. In the subsequent chapters we will go even more in detail about the social justice system and how it applies to you, the entrepreneur.

2

POSITIVE PROGRAMMING FOR WEALTH

GO ALL OUT

The prophet (SAW) came with the same message as Moses and Jesus (AS) were sent with. He was sent to all humanity. And this is a critical point because it makes the Muslim transcend race, gender and geographical location. The message is for all people. Even non-Muslims benefit greatly from the mercy of Islam.

That was how, for the first time ever in history, the Muslims globalized trade. Someone could have a business spanning from China, to Spain, to West Africa. Talk about true globalization!

So Islam promotes trade for everyone. The laws of the Shariah (sacred laws) protects everyone's wealth and property. This is all to promote prosperity. Even during Hajj in Makkah, merchants are selling.

To this day, you will find people engaged in trade while going around the Kaa'ba. Someone could be trying to sell a nice watch to you while you are going around the Kaa'ba! And this is perfectly allowed. Islam allows you that much room and freedom to make profits. Obviously, the purpose of Hajj is not trade but trade is still allowed.

YOUR SPECIAL CONNECTION

First of all, the Muslim Entrepreneur views himself as the slave of Allah. The slave is the highest spiritual rank the messengers reached. Why is that?

For you as an entrepreneur, being a slave of Allah means that you are following the Natural Process. This natural process is the order Allah has put on this earth. That is He provides, and we take. Just like the birds, you too rely on Allah for your sustenance.

The bird wakes up hungry and then goes back in the evening with a full stomach. Unfortunately most of us are conditioned to depend on the government or other people to provide us with food and other necessities. And that is not the Natural Process. It breeds into us fear and insecurity.

I have always been amazed to see that some people who have very little are so peaceful. Yet I was even more amazed to see people with a lot of wealth, not worried in the least over losing it.

Like Mujeeb Ur Rahman, CEO of REDCO, who lost his multi-million dollar construction business when he was implicated falsely and put in jail. He did not mind the loss, which is why he was able to build it up again from scratch when he got out.

Another great entrepreneur I think of is Dr. Yaqub Mirza, CEO of Sterling Management Group, Inc in North America. When I first met him, I was struck by the calmness in his face and his voice. I later learnt he had this calmness despite having under his management assets worth over $3 billion.

THE PEN WROTE IN YOUR FAVOUR

In some discussions, people have viewed Qadr as fate. This is a misunderstanding. Someone who understands this concept will know Entrepreneurship and Qadr are very much linked.

Our Creator is in control and He gave us enough abilities to succeed. Believing that will give you a naturally peaceful and easy going attitude.

Have you ever seen a gloomy negative child? When was the last time you have seen a child with no big dreams? You've probably never seen such a child, no matter what their background is.

That is because every human is born with a natural disposition of doing good and trusting in God. It is after we age that we become fearful. I experienced that myself.

I am cheerful by nature, but if I ever hang around gloomy, negative and pessimistic people long enough, something bad would rub off on me, too!

Remember, a child is not worried about eating tomorrow. He is just enjoying the present moment. As adults, we can do the same. We believe that we will be provided for through our businesses. And everything will be fine.

READ!

The first command to the Muslim is to read and acquire knowledge. As the ayah says :

"Read in the name of your Lord who created."

- Al-Quran, Surah Al-Alaq, Ayah 1

Knowledge is very important for the person who wants to succeed. Islam is truly a religion of learning. For example, at one point in time, the Muslims faced difficulties in dividing the inheritance properly. This was especially the case when the family of the defunct was large. The Quran goes into detail as to the share of each inheritor but the cases are numerous. That pushed some Muslims to develop what we call Algebraic Equations today.

So; how will you know where to go to if you do not know the destination or the road that leads to it?

Know that success comes readily when you learn the right information and think the right way about your business. By reading this book, you will learn about the principles of success as applied by Muslim Entrepreneurs. The good news is that you can learn these principles and apply them in your life.

Many of the entrepreneurs I interviewed learnt success skills at a young age. Some other successful Muslim Entrepreneurs learnt their skills by themselves and were able to create their own empires. This book is going to show you what they know and how you can use it further to build your own success.

What is wonderful is that most information is accessible to everyone nowadays. The ground is level, so to speak! You just have to know where to look for the information and how to use it. By the end of this book, you will know how to do both.

SPREAD THE WEALTH

Let's start with the end in mind. So you've got your business; and you've become successful. What do you do next?

What should you do with all that money?

The answer is simple; spread the goods. Spread the blessings around you. Imagine putting a smile on all those faces. Did you know there is nothing less than a great reward in the Hereafter for someone who puts a smile on another Muslim's face?

Imagine all those prayers. Imagine all those transformed lives. Imagine your new community. Their prayers and gratitude will bless and increase your wealth.

Farouk Sheikh is a Muslim Entrepreneur at the head of several multi-million dollar enterprises. Born in Kenya, he first started his ventures in the import-export field. After moving to the U.S, he now owns multiple ventures that span from technology to real estate to investment.

One of Farouk's business practices is to make the most social impact he can. On one occasion, he was developing an existing residential area in Ohio, U.S.A. Now the area was run down. Properties had broken fences and missing windows. So he did the landscaping for the entire neighbourhood, not just his property. He went as far as to repair fences and plant flowers on the sidewalks.

This had the desired affect. It motivated other homeowners to take better care of their property. The result was the entire area went up in market value.

Now for a person that is only driven by profit, Farouk's move may seem to be a wasteful expenditure in the short-term. But in the long run, he won big time. His property went up in value. His neighbours loved him. Everybody welcomed his contribution. It was a win-win situation all around.

Now that is a Muslim Entrepreneur in action! You light up people's faces, transform their lives and profit greatly at the same time.

Remember: give your money and time in a way that people can prosper. You'll find you won't decrease in either. What you give will most definitely come back to you.

Whatever country you are in, be concerned about the people around you. As the saying goes :

"When you cut down a tree, plant another one."

-Dr. Hany Al-Banna, Founder of Islamic Relief

Dr. Hany is the man behind one of the world's biggest charity foundations, Islamic Relief.

Besides the advantages mentioned above, there is also an unmatched satisfaction when you give back. Simply making a profit does not provide this satisfaction.

I invite you to meditate on Allah's creation. The lion hunts and eats the antelopes but then he ages and dies, decomposes into the soil and is eaten by another antelope. In the same way, our Creator allows us to trade and make a great profit. After the profit is made, it is natural to give back. In this way, society will run smoothly, in balance.

3

THE DUAL ADVANTAGE

THE BEST WEAPON

Du'a gives results. And fast!

The companions of the prophet (SAW) used to ask Allah for everything; from winning battles to getting new shoelaces.

As Allah says in the Quran:

"And when My servants ask you, [O Muhammad], concerning Me – indeed I am near. I respond to the invocation of the supplicant when he calls upon Me."

- Al-Quran, Surah Al-Baqarah, Ayah 186

So your best weapon is du'a. You see, asking takes the pressure off of you. This will come in handy given that in your pursuit of success, you will naturally encounter a number of setbacks. What will you do then?

The Quran instructs that you and I will persevere. Yet if you feel like success is 100% dependent on you, then lack of success can feel like a burden.

Take the example of the employee that just got laid off.
There are two attitudes he could adopt:

1- "This is all so-and-so's fault." With this attitude, there is always somebody else to blame. Either the boss, the company, the spouse or their own selves.

2- "I have a part to play in my own success. But in the end, the result depends on God." This is the attitude that helps a Muslim to persevere.

Like a miracle, the pressure is completely released.

WORSHIP THROUGH WEALTH

We now know that du'a is a great tool for your success. This is whilst you rely on Allah for the results you want. Now we get down to work.

You see, work brings prosperity. Work is virtuous. Work is encouraged. To reap, the farmer has to sow.

You are encouraged to meditate on this natural process over and over again in the Quran. Look at the farmer. He plants first, then waits for the rain to grow his crops. The same applies to you! Do the work first, then wait for Allah to deliver the results.

A grain is needed to expect a harvest. As a Muslim Entrepreneur, all you do is plant, and then expect a good crop. It's that simple!

You are not expected to plant, bring about the rain and make the seed break into roots by yourself. You rely on Allah for the results. Forget about the outcome. Just plant some good seeds!

CONTROL SWITCH

As a Muslim Entrepreneur, you believe that "everything will be alright. My business will grow. I will have customers." You have no choice but to believe.

In my discussions on theology with Muslim scholars, I learnt that Allah created the Pen that wrote down exactly what will happen in the future.

That just shows that He is not bound by time.
He knows what will happen but that does not influence us in our decisionmaking. It is just reassurance that what happens is ultimately good and doing our best is good enough.

Art Willams said this: "All I can do is all I can do. And all I can do is enough." Do your best and everything will be taken care of.

Don't try to predict the future. That is what leads to gambling in business and in the stock market.

WIN TODAY AND TOMORROW

You probably already know that this life is but a passing moment. Most of us don't live to be 100 years old. The next life is more important and lasts forever. But does it mean that this life has no importance?

No. It is a testing ground to see who does the most good.
For you, to be an entrepreneur is about solving problems and improving other people's lives. That being said, wealth is a measure of the service you render to society. The more value you give to people in their lives, the more you will be paid. That is why the reward can be enormous.

So each and every one of you is potentially an entrepreneur. You just have to find a way to serve the people, improve their lives or experiences and you will prosper. How much you succeed depends only on how many people you serve.

In my interviews, I met some of the most generous individuals. They are generous with their time, money and are also passionate about sharing their knowledge. They are always giving back.

ZAKAT SPREADS WEALTH

Zakat is charged on any wealth you're not using.

Say you have money just sitting there in your bank account. 2.5% of that money is then given in zakat. It goes to mostly people in need; either the poor or those in debt.

Unused wealth in Islam has to be distributed, not hoarded.

Say you're a successful Muslim Entrepreneur. You decide to use your wealth to build a company or invest the money in another entrepreneur's company. You're putting your money to work. There is no zakat due on this money as long as you are reinvesting the money. Now isn't that nice? It means entrepreneurship strives in a free market following Islamic principles.

Say you want to keep $10,000 in your bank (or under your mattress). If you paid the zakat due on those savings, you would lose almost $4,600 of that money over a 25-year period. That's almost half of your savings gone!

That is huge. Could you avoid losing that much? Absolutely. By making your money work for you. You could either start a business, or invest in someone else's business. Those not following this Islamic principle are at a disadvantage when it comes to entrepreneurship.

You see the prevailing economic system encourages you to hoard wealth. You are rewarded for keeping your money stagnant instead of making it work. This is what interest is all about.

In Islam, what you have instead is a system that rewards calculated risk-taking instead of hoping your wealth grows because of interest.

As a Muslim, this is good news for you! You're actually obeying Allah when you do what grows your money and community in the fastest way possible. See how your religion enjoins you to be prosperous?

THE NEED FOR A SUCCESS PHILOSOPHY

1

WHAT BRINGS SUCCESS

MUSLIMS : GET RICH!

All of us humans are on a mission assigned to us by our Creator. From amongst mankind, the Muslim has a special place because he is using divine principles to further his material and spiritual needs on Earth.

You see, in Islam we don't just live for either the soul, the body or the mind. For example, you can get closer to Allah SWT by getting married. You draw closer still by acquiring wealth and spending it to please our Creator. This is the balanced, middle path of Islam. As the balanced religion, Allah SWT does want you to have things, but in order to glorify Him.

Wealth is therefore essential for you.

Yet people ask me: "why should I strive to have more and be more?"
My reply is simple: in order to eat good food, drink good water, live in a nice place and cultivate your spirit with books and travel.

These things you can only do with wealth.

The other reason why you want to be wealthy is so that you can give. How often are we told to give in charity in the Quran? But I want you to think about it this way: how will you give if you do not have?

That is why in a famous incident, the prophet SAW made clear the superiority of the wealthy, strong and righteous sahaba over the rest.

You see, Madinah was the city of immigration for Muslims that were being persecuted. They left their homes and properties to practice their faith. Some of those poor Muslims were known as the people of Suffa – meaning they slept in the Masjid. At the same time, some other companions were extremely wealthy and could spend freely in charity. The poor people of Suffa could not.

The poor from the companions – may Allah be pleased with them - came to the prophet SAW and complained about their situation:

"The rich pray just like us, do battle when we do yet they have an advantage. They spend while we cannot," they said.

Now I want you to think about yourself. How many times did you want to give, but you could not?

Back to the story; the prophet SAW gave the Suffa some invocations (dhikr) to do in order to catch up in reward with the wealthier sahaba. However, the rich sahaba heard about that and started doing the same dhikr. When the suffa protested, the prophet SAW said that this was a bounty from Allah.

He favours some people over others.

The other reason you want to be wealthy is so that you can invest in ideas. I am certain that on at least one occasion, you've said to yourself: if only I had the money, I would build this and that or invest in that or the other. It is only by having financial abundance that you can invest in ideas and projects.

Now to have this abundance in wealth, you must first have an abundance in mind. That is positive self belief; that is to be optimistic.

HOW TO PLAY THE GAME?

Success can be evasive. Sometimes, you might try hard to get something but every time you get close to it, it escapes you. It could be a goal you had or something you wanted to get. But it keeps evading you. Have you ever wondered why?

It is because of readiness. The good that you desire can come at any time, but you need to be ready to receive it. Success will come but only at the right time. Success is never late nor is it early. It is always right on time.
And if you are not ready and become rich then it is very likely that you will lose it all and never regain it.

You see this happen all the time. Lottery winners are a good example. Within five years, they tend to lose all the millions acquired through gambling. We see the same situation with people that become wealthy through government corruption and not entrepreneurship.

So in your process of acquiring wealth and success, if you experience failures, just assume that you are not ready for it. Improve yourself so that you are ready when success shows up.

The second factor that will allow you to reach your full potential is to position yourself for success.

Think about it this way: if your goal is to become a great entrepreneur and reach financial success, you've got to start a business. It seems obvious; but so many would-be entrepreneurs miss this part! They never get started.

The last important factor that prevents most people from success is just their lack of knowledge.
If you don't know what you are doing, or where you are going, it might be difficult for you to get there. Sometimes you just don't know what you don't know. And if you knew you would get there faster.

So the smart thing to do is to ask people that have been there and know the road to success. You are going to meet some of them in this book and learn exactly what they did to get great results.

ECONOMIC FUEL

Giving Zakat is compulsory (fard). It's one of the five pillars of Islam. The first pillar of Islam is the shahada, which is a declaration of the correct belief in Allah and His messenger SAW. The shahada will give you the correct belief that will bring real, lasting success.

Because you're now depending on your true Provider, the Creator of everything. You believe with certainty that you will be provided for and that you will follow the prophetic example of living.

The second pillar is Salah (prayer). It is a devotional connection with your Creator performed 5 times a day. As an entrepreneur, Allah is also the Provider that will give you all you need for your sustenance. What you want to buy, where you want to live; all comes from Allah, your one source.

Then there is Zakat. Zakat is the giving to the needy of excess wealth you're not using in a productive manner. For example, if someone has savings just sitting there, then 2.5% of that money is due to people that need it more. This includes the poor, people traveling, and people that are sick, to name a few. There is an entire body of religious knowledge dealing with the rulings of zakat. It's the noblest act of worship after prayer. The number of times it has been mentioned in the Quran equates the number of times salat has been mentioned.

But one must understand that if there is no surplus wealth, there is no zakat. If you are using all your money right now to pay the bills or to cover your basic expenses, there is no zakat due at all.

You are encouraged to have more wealth because that surplus will enable you to pay zakat and the poor can be taken care of. So remember: Zakat is dependent on surplus of wealth, production and resources.

No surplus, no zakat. Zakat is right after prayer, and that's how important success is in this life, because it allows you to give zakat, a huge act of worship. For the business owner it is easier to have this surplus than the employee, who rarely has wealth sitting around.

It is surprising: Zakat really encourages you to be wealthy and be all you can be.

THE 10-33% RULE

There are things you can do to drastically improve your chances as an entrepreneur.

One such thing is simply this:

"If you want more, give more!"

If your parents are still alive, then you are in for a treat! You can make them happy and this will have a direct effect on your results. So make it a goal to commit a part of your income to your parents. If they are not alive anymore, you can still do hajj for them.

Charity (sadaqa) is also a big factor to improve your chances. According to Imam Ashraf, the founder of NTG Clarity Networks Inc. , if you donate 10% of your income to sadaqa then your business will never go down. How is that for a plan?

And it matters even more when things are tight!

You might say: "Oumar, I don't have a business right now. Not going down is not good enough! I want to go up, exponentially fast!"

The solution is charity again: donate 33% of your income, and things will permanently go up.

Now, there are also things to avoid. It is great to do the good and this will naturally make you avoid the bad. However, the entrepreneur might forget and fall into forbidden things.

I will cite the most important things to avoid in order for you to be successful as a Muslim Entrepreneur.

The first thing is Ribaa, most commonly in the form of interest. In the chapter on Wealth Building Strategies, we will see how Muslim Entrepreneurs are able to achieve great wealth through investments and partnerships instead of interest.

The second thing to avoid is romantic relationships outside of marriage. They spread disease, mistrust and poverty in the society. "The Power of the Group" chapter will show you an alternative. Marriage with the right man or woman can really make you strive and succeed.

YOUR TRUE CALLING

In Islam, the goal is to worship our creator, Allah.

The Quran says:

"And I did not create the jinn and mankind except to worship Me. I do not want from them any provision, nor do I want them to feed Me."

-Al-Quran, Surah Adh-Dhariyat, Ayah 56-57

This is an oft-quoted ayah. We must remember whilst reading this ayah that production and success are part of worship, if done with Ehsaan. Ehsaan means doing it in the best way, with the right intention. We will discuss this in a later chapter on work ethics.

Now you have to understand that producing something valuable for the society around you is worship. Having success in that is worship.
Sheikh Said told me something amazing about surah Doha where Allah says:

"And as for the favor of your Lord, proclaim it."

-Al-Quran, Surah Ad-Duhaa, Ayah 11

He explained that in economic terms, this means if you become a millionaire or very successful, then let it be known! That way, people remember God's favour through you. That way they know who to come to for help. This is also a part of worship.

Remember, the prophet (SAW) was ordered to say:

"Indeed, my prayer, my rites of sacrifice, my living and my dying are for Allah, Lord of the worlds."

-Al-Quran, Surah Al-Anam, Ayah 162

So everything the Muslim entrepreneur is doing is worship, as long as it's halal. There is no contradiction between worship and success in this life.

Having an amazing relationship with your wife is worship. Having children is worship. Having a nice house is worship. That is why Islam is a beautiful way of life. It allows you to achieve success holistically. It allows you to believe that by achieving success, you are really engaging in worship.

Now if everything we do can be worship, the question remains, what does Allah intend for you specifically? This question requires self-assessment; assessing your own personality and deciding for yourself. What do you enjoy doing the most? As you will see in the chapter on Critical Skills, to truly become a great entrepreneur you will need to acquire a high level of skills. It will be important to find out what your calling is so you start acquiring those skills immediately. Your time and energy are too valuable to waste.

HIDDEN TREASURE

Every day, people write books on leadership, relationship building, money- these are categories of success. These books will teach you how to make profit, how to benefit from the stock market, how to start successful relationships and maintain them. These areas have been covered extensively. But very little has been written about those fields using the right spiritual values – Islamic values. The treasure of knowledge that the Messenger SAW and Muslim scholars left us has not yet been exploited to its full potential.

Some books have been written on trade, but the focus was not on corporations, making profit or being successful in today's context.

On the Western side of things, there is a lot of guesswork when it comes to spirituality. It is mostly New Age. New religions are cropping up that put God aside and talk about "Nature" and "The Universe" instead. Now, there may be initial benefit in coming from that angle, but when Allah's guidance is ignored, we will see error down the line.

What you have here in this book is special. Islam does justice to our lives in both worlds. I want you to aim for the next life, whilst being successful in this one.

Remember, Makkah was a city of traders; the Quraysh were wealthy and made large profits. The prophet SAW was himself a successful entrepreneur. Thus, I can say without being biased that Islam is the perfect spirituality for asking 'what is success?' and 'how do I achieve it?'

That is why we want to know what the Muslim Entrepreneurs are practicing to achieve success. What is working for them today? What is their mode of thinking?

2

SUCCESS IS LEARNABLE

THE BILLIONAIRE BUS DRIVER

I have great news for you; success is learnable. If you are not successful right now, or want to go to the next level in your success, then know that success is like learning how to drive.

The first time I was behind the wheel, I was scared! It was very uncomfortable; you don't know if you're in lane, and cars are going by super fast! So I had this fear of driving. But, once I learnt the skill, it became very easy. You just sit back and go on autopilot. It just flows.

The same way, when you start your enterprise, in the beginning it may seem difficult or undoable. You may even wonder how on earth some people are doing it? For some entrepreneurs, business success seems like a habit. They are always achieving goals and producing good work, whatever their field is. Know this: successful people are not born that way. They are developed. And you can learn the same. Just like driving. You can always become more; more intelligent, more knowledgeable, more disciplined. You can always do more.

More good things, for this life and the hereafter. If you have that attitude, you can always go to the next level.

What you have to realize is that we all have a lot of potential. Not just the Muslim Entrepreneur. Any baby that is born is a blank canvas. And they have the knowledge to learn. A baby doesn't know anything other than that they can learn. And that is the biggest kind of knowing.

For example, a baby will never think "I can't walk! I can't speak!" They know they can! Because they see others around them doing it. They have the knowledge that if people like them know how to do something, they can do it too. Even if they have to do it over and over again. Eventually they learn how to walk and talk.

In the same way, for you as a Muslim Entrepreneur you have a lot of potential. Many people before you have faced the exact same challenges. Whether it's paying the bills or keeping up with your business expenses, know that millions before you had the same problem. And they solved it.

Sir Anwar Pervez was once a simple bus driver in Bradford, England. He eventually went into business for himself and is now a billionaire. He is not worried about bills anymore. My hope for you is that you learn from the people that overcame the same kind of issues you might have now. Just apply the same principles. And guess what? You'll get the same results!

THREE LITTLE PRINCESSES

As a Muslim Entrepreneur, you know that when you teach good things, you share the reward of the good that comes as a result.

For example, if you teach many people how to become wealthy, successful and how to invest, you too will have wealthier people around you. This is really useful. Imagine one day you yourself need help or an associate to go into business with you. If all of your contacts were poor, then good luck! But if a fair amount are successful, you will benefit. This is the immediate benefit. But in Islam, we go to the next level.

By impacting other people, you get rewarded in the hereafter as well. Whoever does a good deed will see the reward in both lives. It is a very powerful concept.

The second reason is that you do it to have more prosperity for yourself. As Muslims we spread the good because Allah's bounties are infinite. That way we end up becoming very prosperous. We're not worried that Allah's supply is finite.

You see, there is this misconception that resources on Earth are finite. That we cannot have more, that we need less people. That is a scarcity mindset. And it is very damaging. It is being taught in schools around the globe. Know that whoever Allah creates, He puts their rizq in front of them. It's all calculated; sent down in the right proportion. So He will provide enough resources. Enough crops. Enough rain.

Enough gold. Enough technology; to accommodate all the people that are on Earth. The supply really is infinite. It's Allah who creates and His promise is that He will provide for us all.

You don't have to worry about what other people get. They are not going to take all the riches for themselves! Know that the wealth is infinite. It increases as people increase. You don't lose anything by teaching your brother how to become wealthy and successful. You're not in competition with anybody but yourself for your sustenance (rizq).

If you do what you're supposed to do; following the principles in this book, you will get wealthy. No matter what other people do. And it will really be to your benefit to teach other people to prosper.

The third reason you want to teach success and good things is because you will learn more. You see, in my career as a doctorate researcher, one of my jobs was to teach. And I can tell you that teaching is something very beautiful. The more you teach, the more you learn.

I had a similar experience in my coaching. I was mentoring Mamadou Tidiane Diop about how to set up his online marketing business and build an audience for himself. He learnt a lot about personal development, which was new to him. He started dreaming again. As a new father of triplets who are all daughters, he built his belief about providing well for his new family and help others in the process. He thanked me for encouraging him to pursue his goals. I can tell you that just by teaching that subject, I mastered it ten times more.

That is why teaching is so beautiful.

Your knowledge increases as you teach. So teach success. Share the good.

Give someone this book! Seek good advice. Give good advice yourself. And watch people prosper. You will see people prosper around you, because again, the bounties of your Lord are infinite!

BUILD DON'T BURN

Instead of criticising, add to knowledge. You see, success has been studied for hundreds, if not thousands of years. There is a huge body of knowledge available already. People in the East have studied it. We have 'Kitaab ul Amwaal' (the Book of Wealth) written by Abu Ibn Jafar Al Daudi in Arabic 1,000 years ago.

In recent years, the West has pushed it even further. In the early 20th century, the American author Napoleon Hill wrote his famous book 'Think and Grow Rich'. These are tremendous books for success, wealth and prosperity.

Napolean Hill started a trend of self-help that has been extremely popular since. If you read Personal Development books, you'll agree. Yet to my knowledge, this book here is the first of its kind that gives a Muslim perspective on wealth and success in recent times.

Now does that mean the information that already exists on success building from outside of Muslim scholarship is 100% false? No! Not at all. The majority of it is accurate in my opinion.

But why not go to the next level? What we want to do is add to the knowledge instead of criticizing and destroying what already exists.

The goal is not to just do our own thing alone. It's to impact a lot of people, no matter where they are from, and benefit all of humanity because that's what being a Muslim is all about.

If we want to study what Islam says about wealth, then we must study under Muslim entrepreneurs who have already achieved success. That is taking the success philosophy to the next level. In this book, I've avoided textbook knowledge to the best of my ability and instead given you what is working today for so many amazing Muslim entrepreneurs and leaders. Eventually, the lessons you learn here can be applied to every field; even beyond your business.

I end this section by reminding you that inferiority is inherent in criticism. For example, if other people have already written thousands of books, it's just not useful to destroy everything. You can learn from the other. What's required for the Muslim Entrepreneur is to discern between what's useful and what's not. Only the inferior person will say 'you're not doing anything right!' A superior mind will use what already works and make it better.

When I first met Shahzad Siddiqi, a young thirty-something successful lawyer, he was studying the biography of US president Lincoln. He told me he is looking for some principles that Lincoln applied to go from being a person that ventured through multiple businesses with zero success to president. Shahzad himself has also authored three books on Islamic finance.

3

THE MUSLIM MILLIONAIRE MINDSET

WHERE ARE SUCCESSFUL MUSLIMS?

They are everywhere. All around you.

I've seen people with a very high net worth in Africa. Extremely wealthy. I'm thinking of Mr. Aliko Dangote who is worth over $20 billion. He was educated in Al Azhar University, Egypt and is the wealthiest African entrepreneur alive.

I've seen people in North America becoming very wealthy. I think of Dr. Yaqub Mirza: the investor, and the Mirza brothers in Internet marketing. I think about Azim Rizvee in property development and real estate.

I'm thinking about many other individuals, like the Zaghloul brothers who are building tremendous businesses in Canada and Egypt, and who were able to take over ten businesses public.

I'm thinking about people in Turkey like Mrs. Selva Gurdogan, whose architecture firm Superpool is world renowned. I'm thinking of Dr. Amina Coxon, the physician on Harley Street, London.

I'm thinking about people in Pakistan, like Shahid Tata, who runs a major textile business: the TATA corporation. I'm thinking of the founders of REDCO in Doha, the Rahman brothers. I'm thinking of Senegal, where Mr. Jamil owns food production chains. He started with just a roadside table in Dakar and moved up to a shop. Now he owns large production chains for processing and packaging food.

From Africa to Asia, to North America to Oceania. You name it, they're there! Many Muslim entrepreneurs are becoming very wealthy and having a big impact on people.

Muslim Entrepreneurs are winning wherever they go. They are applying the principles of revelation and they have an advantage.

Now, here and there you will have some discrepancies. In some cases, tyrants and unfair people can temporarily block the roadway to success. But know that the Earth is vast. Some people migrate. Some stay in their countries of origin. So is there a specific place to become wealthy?

No.

Wherever you are, you can become wealthy there.
Provided there is no war, because you cannot build a factory in unstable circumstances. But in fairly stable circumstances, yes you can become successful.

Yes, you can become wealthy. Read the book 'Acres of Diamonds' by Russell Conwell to build your belief on finding wealth no matter where you are.

Now where do Muslim Entrepreneurs stand compared to the rest? They are among the wealthiest on earth. Again, Aliko Dangote is worth over $20 billion. Mr. Premji in India is also worth over $20 billion. In the Arabian peninsula, prince Al Waleed Bin Talal recently made the news by pledging to give over $30 billion of his wealth in charity.

So they stand very high on the pedestal of success. Has it always been like that? Yes! In the past too, Muslims have been very wealthy.

Take the example of Mansa Musa, the Muslim king of the empire of Mali, West Africa. He set out to do hajj with 60,000 of his followers. They stopped in Cairo on the way to Makkah and gave away so much gold in charity that the Cairo gold market crashed for the next two hundred years.

So, success is everywhere. In every generation. And know that other people like yourself have been through the roadway of success. You can do it, if they can do it. And this is good news for you!

KEEP IT PURE

The concept of Niyyah in Islam gives us an edge on success. It teaches us how to have the right intention, how to do an action that's good, and how to achieve success in the quickest way possible.

Have you ever felt bad, angry, had fear, frustration or worry? That kind of emotion is usually created by the wrong kind of thinking, Thoughts like "God is not going to provide for me, there is not enough out there, or I'm going to fail" are all negative thoughts. That kind of thinking is paralyzing. People that have that kind of thinking are rarely successful at all.

I did an exam once, and I had the wrong thinking. So I was very stressed out, and I performed poorly as compared to my usual standards, even though I passed. In another exam I was really relaxed, I had the right thinking, and I outperformed everyone else. Why was I stressed at my first exam? Because I tried to control in my mind what I could not control: the future.

This is true everywhere you go. If you think the right thing and perform the right action, you will have the right results. In your business, in your life, in everything you do. Islam teaches you to do the right thing with the right intention.

So your intention can be; "I want to work with this company; I want to make this amount of money."

For what purpose? The chain of thinking could be: "to feed my family; to give to those that have less; to live in a better environment; to go to hajj; to please my parents; to please Allah." As long as in the end, it is to please Allah. Determine what the right intention is for you and watch what happens to your results.

THE RICH THINK DIFFERENTLY

Being poor is an attitude. Being rich is also an attitude.

The Quran talks about those virtuous Muslims that you can recognize because they are poor yet they don't ask. You see, there is nothing wrong in not having money and means; millions are in this situation. Temporary poverty is fine; what is dangerous is permanent poverty. That is, when someone decides they will be poor forever. Being poor is a state of mind. It is to say "I am poor and that is it. There are no riches for me."

So what is the difference between the rich Muslim Entrepreneur and the poor, average and ordinary?

The main difference is that the rich think bigger. For the sake of examples, I will give monetary figures in American dollars. If you think you are worth $50,000 per annum, then you will most likely study hard and become an engineer or something similar. Then you'll end up making that kind of money.

If you think you are worth $300,000, then it would be natural to look into becoming an athlete, a surgeon or similar. If you think even bigger, you'll probably go into manufacturing and have a factory – you get the picture?

If you think you are a billionaire, you are probably building hotels or building huge corporations. You are just constantly doing and doing.

As you can see, it is a matter of belief. So think about it this way and you will prosper in your business. Even if you are working for someone else right now, the money you earn will reflect what you believe you are worth.

You are exactly what you believe you are worth. Not a penny more, not a penny less.

For example, did you notice that you always have around the same amount of money left at the end of the month? If right now you're earning, lets say $50,000 a year. Do you notice that you tend to earn that kind of money consistently? Even if you lose your job, you tend to get back to something around that area.

That is because it's very difficult for someone used to earning $50,000 a year to go down to a consistent earning of $20,000. They believe they are worth $50,000. Some people believe they're worth $500,000 a year. And they're earning it. If those people earn only $50,000 a year, they feel broke! So they do enough to make the kind of money they're used to.

It's no different for your business. If you really believe that you will succeed, you will tend to succeed. That is why my recommendation for you is to think big. Think bigger. Have high ambitions, high dreams. And that's one of the characteristics of the believer.

I heard Imam Said Rageah mention a very prominent Islamic personality. He was known as the fifth Caliph for his righteousness.

He was from a very wealthy family. He was the leader of the Muslims around 100 years after the prophet SAW.

His name was Umar Ibn Abd Al Aziz and was quoted saying "I have a soul that is always aiming high." That is because as a young man, he wanted to marry Fatima, a prominent noble lady of strong heritage and great beauty. He went for it and he married her.

Then he wanted to become a governor. And he became a governor. Then he wanted to become the ruler of the country. And he became the Caliph. As he grew older and death was approaching, he said: "My soul aims high and I hope I will reach jannatul firdaus (the highest level of paradise)."

That is the attitude of the Muslim. Aim high, for this life and the hereafter. Develop that attitude. It distinguishes the very successful from the average and the ordinary. Become a big thinker, and you will see big results.

PRINCIPLE III

ATTITUDE

1

PROMOTE THE GOOD

THE OPTIMIST'S RELIGION

The first asset of the Muslim Entrepreneur is his optimism. I had the opportunity to interview a great entrepreneur; Mrs. Oumou Ndiaye.

She is the owner of a Senegal based company that develops software for customs companies and governments. Born and raised in Senegal, she went to France to study Applied Mathematics before returning home. All the African market was dominated by European and North American companies. Yet, she said to herself:

"I studied in the same universities as these people and I know the African context better than these foreign companies. I believe I can do this."

-Oumou Ndiaye, CEO ModelSiS

She was able to beat the competition both in price and quality and secured her first major contract. The rest is history. Today she does business with several African countries and is planning to get into the European and Asian markets. The key is that she believed in herself and was optimistic about the situation, despite the heavy competition she faced.

So as a Muslim Entrepreneur, make sure you keep you spirits high. Don't give up when the going gets tough. Rather, cultivate optimism. Believe that Allah SWT, who created you out of nothing, is fully aware of your situation and will help you.

There is a second source for the Muslim Entrepreneur's optimism after the belief in Allah. It is the repeated Quranic encouragement of spreading good news and avoid spreading the bad.

As a Muslim, you have to always assume good. Again this is part of the prophetic character. The prophet SAW told his companions not to tell him about the faults of their brothers because that might lead him to think ill of the person the next time they met.

Now imagine all the negativity you see on TV these days. Especially about our own brothers and sisters.

It is hard to get a good opinion of people after watching them do bad things. That is why most Muslim Entrepreneurs I interviewed don't waste time watching TV. If they do, it is only for a few minutes at a time in order to follow their particular trade.

I am not saying that watching TV is bad. It is bad if you have a big dream!

BUILD TRUST

It is just a representation of what the prophet (SAW) was all about; perseverance, courage, virtue, and above all else, integrity, truthfulness and trustworthiness. Being trustworthy (al-ameen) was one of the prophet (SAW)'s names. You can see this quality reflected in his companions too, like Abu Bakr who was also known as the truthful one (al-sadeeq). It is a non-wavering way of being. It's straightforward. That's what makes it a universally important characteristic trait.

I remember hearing Warren Buffett, the most successful American investor alive today, saying his entire business as well as the entire financial system is based on trust. Why? Because you're not going to do a financial transaction if you don't trust that the other person will deliver on what they said they will.

In the same manner, I learnt from Dr. Yaqub Mirza, CEO of the Amanah Mutual Fund, that trust and integrity were the major factors for success. The way you deal with people is important. Dr. Mirza was raised by his entrepreneurial father and he learnt the art of negotiation and deal making from him. One time he was negotiating a deal with a company in Zimbabwe. He used some of his advanced negotiation skills. Very quickly, he started to overpower the other side.

He realized he could take advantage of the other person but did not because he remembered that he got to be fair and just. So he stopped.

That is integrity! And this kind of behaviour made his investment company attract over 3 billion dollars in assets.

Dr. Ike Ahmed, running a major eye centre in Canada, and a world-class expert on glaucoma, has a thriving business seeing 600 patients per day. One of his strategies of building trust is by being honest and straightforward with his patients. If they don't need surgery, they're told so. He doesn't pocket the money.

What you have to understand is, your character will eventually define what your destiny is. So how do you develop that prophetic character? It's all based on what you believe. What your daily actions are. So the Muslim character is a character that is solely dependent on Allah. Remember that everything is already written. You cannot get a penny more, by cheating or whining or doing anything fraudulent. You will get every penny that was written for you. It is a very powerful concept. All you will have is all you will have.

The Muslim Character is also positive; very positive and uplifting. So convey the positive things you hear and refrain from the bad. Don't push people away from you. That's one of the recommendations of the prophet (SAW). If you want to build your enterprise and be successful, follow these basic principles. They will lead you to success no matter where you are or what occupation you have.

KEEP SMILING

In the realm of success, your perspective is very important. If you view that something is negative then it will be, and it will affect your performance. If you think it's positive, then it will be. Now how does this relate to Islam and the positive attitude of the Muslim entrepreneur?

The prophet (SAW) said:

"Make things easy for people and not difficult. Give people good news and bring them joy, and do not turn them away…"

That's one of the fundamental principles; that you believe that Allah wants ease for you. You believe that whatever is going on right now in your life, all the challenges in your business and personal relationships, are all from Allah. And here I want to cite Mujeeb Ur Rahman (CEO of REDCO in Doha). He came from a business family. Right after college graduation, he decided to go into the lucrative Qatari construction business with his brother. He put in the young company the same enthusiasm he had as former captain of the University Hockey team. He worked hard and the business grew exponentially.

However things turned around when they became too big and politicians tried to take them down. The two brothers were imprisoned. Mujeeb faced tremendous life threatening difficulties, but he remembered the Quran and the examples of the prophets like Yusuf AS.

If you hold on to that, at the end of the day you will succeed. Today, Mujeeb Ur Rahman is back into business and he maintains a radiant face due to his positive belief in Allah.

The prophet SAW was known for smiling. He was always smiling, upbeat and full of energy. That attitude really affected everyone around him.

Do the same! No matter what's going on, just view it as positive, smile it off and move forward. Keep going! And you'll succeed.

LIKE IT OR LOVE IT

On your way to success, you'll see that the emotion of gratitude is one of the most important characteristic traits for success.

First of all, you want to know where you are. Ask yourself, where am I really? Am I really that poor? How am I doing? If you know how to read, have a cell phone right now, the internet and a laptop, you are privileged. On top of all that, if you have the greatest blessings of all, which is faith in Allah, then you are one of the lucky few. If you have reasonable health, then be grateful. So be grateful no matter what's going on.

Say to yourself, "I am so happy and grateful to Allah that I have such and such." It is essentially "Alhamdulillah" in Arabic, we say it all the time in prayer.

One good way to remember the blessings you have is to put a list of ten of them on a piece of paper and place it where you can see it everyday. This way you can be grateful for where you are.

If you have a job right now, even if you don't like certain aspects of the job, be grateful for it. I know you want to be an entrepreneur, but having a job is fantastic for now. Be grateful for it! Millions and millions of people are looking for jobs right now and they don't have any. If you have that, be extremely grateful for your employer and to Allah for that opportunity. And now that you know exactly where you are, the next step for you is to look at where you're going. Look at the destination.

What you want to say next is, "I'm so happy and grateful now that-" and list your goal as if you've already achieved it. So you could say, "I'm so happy and grateful now that I'm a millionaire," or "I'm so happy and grateful now that my company XYZ is successful," whatever your business is. This makes you already content with your situation and now you're open for more opportunities. That's why it's so important to be grateful to Allah for what He has already given you, so you can be open to receiving more. The more grateful you are, the better it is on your way to success.

There is a third reason why being grateful is so crucial to your success. When you are grateful, you are open to opportunities and you see them come at you.
You won't automatically think, "oh this won't work". You're not in a rejecting or pessimistic mode, because you're grateful. Being grateful is also being open; they are linked. Whatever comes at you is good! Thinking like this makes you extremely flexible and open. You can see the opportunities all around you so you can go for it and make the enterprise successful.

IT'S YOUR CALL

Now that you are taking responsibility for your own success, you have become a responsible business leader. You are taking responsibility for your actions, you are not blaming anybody and you are just focused on making things happen. The next step is to develop self-reliance; you rely on your own self for your success.

Remember, It's not up to anyone else. It's not up to the bank, your school, your university, your degrees, your parents or your friends. It's up to you to step into your greatness and become successful.

JUST COLOURED WATER

Your thinking really affects who you are and what kind of results you get. Whether it's in the area of health, wealth, relationships or your connection with Allah, really thoughts affect things.

In other words, the way you think really affects who you are, your results and your body in the physical sense. So if you think that you are sick, you are sick. If you think something bad will happen, it's very likely it will be so. The negative energy really does affect your body.

Have you ever met someone that's really negative? I had a friend I knew for about three years; we had a friendship because he was open and easy to talk to. Yet as our friendship progressed, I noticed he never lost an argument; he was always right. Have you ever met someone like that? I noticed that he also liked to talk badly about other people behind their backs. Very quickly, I started to disassociate myself with him. Why am I telling you this? Because this man is divorced, he is miserable and has terrible health problems. I came to realize that your thinking really affects your results.

I'm not saying just because you're positive, you won't have challenges in life. We have prophets like prophet Ayyub who suffered a terrible illness, poverty, loss of children and other trials for years. The difference is he never complained. He only complained to Allah, and only once, after enduring his trial for many years. It is known in the medical community that half of the science called medicine is just placebo. The doctor will give coloured water to the patient to make him think he is getting a real cure. The amazing thing is that coloured water does cure people. If they believe it will!

It just goes to show how positive the Muslim entrepreneur has to be. So don't attract what they call 'bad luck' on you! 'Bad luck' has nothing to do with luck; our own negative thoughts can just affect us.

Remember, if you fear things like disease and are always consumed in negative thoughts, it's very likely bad will happen to you. But if you're thinking positive and uplifting thoughts and expecting good from Allah, good will happen to you. That's also a tradition of our very noble religion. "Allah says, 'I am as my servant expects Me to be, and I am with him when he remembers me. If he thinks of Me, I think of him.'"

However, the right type of fear can also motivate. Dr. Amina Coxon, the renowned medical doctor speaks highly of the right type of fear.

"Fear motivates me. I had to survive. I didn't have anyone else paying for me to get up in the morning. You have to survive!"

2

YOU AND YOUR ENVIRONMENT

FEAR OF LOSS

Now there is much negative energy out there that you want to avoid no matter what, because they can cost you your success. One of them is fear.

Fear is diverse. It can be fear of loss. There is the story of a lady who had a 7$ watch. She goes to a restaurant and forgets the watch on the table. It took her 2 hours to get back to that restaurant and she spent close to 40$ to retrieve the watch. Now she could have easily gone to the local supermarket and spend 7$ to get the same exact watch with no time and fuel wasted. What motivated her to spend that much time money and energy to get the watch back? It is the fear of loss. By the way, I strongly recommend you use this skill if you want to move people to buy your products. It works like a charm.

Another fear is the fear of old age. Someone might say "no I'm too old and can't start my business". Or "what will happen when I get too old?" Or "no I have to keep a job so I can get full retirement". This leads to procrastination. Remember if you think constantly about being old then you are likely to age quickly yourself! That's hopefully not what you want!

There is also the negative energy from doubt and worry. Worry is really something that will drain all of your energy. As an entrepreneur you want to charge and take massive action. You need positive energy, not the chains of negative energy like fears and worry. These could set back your business by years and years.

What I've seen in all successful Muslim entrepreneurs is that they are people of action. When Mujeeb ur Rahman and his brother were building the family construction business in Qatar, they were working around the clock. They were visiting the construction sites themselves to ask about the needs of the builders and then secure new customers. They had over 1,800 customers in a short period of time thanks to not overthinking things.

Don't let doubt creep into your business. It will blow it up. I know some decisions are crucial and should not be rushed. However, success is attracted to speed.

Now, if you follow these steps, will you always be right?

Sometimes it may still be the wrong decision, but the successful entrepreneur strives to make it right. They study the subject, do their best, and also make sure that the decision is the right one by taking action. Sometimes the window of opportunity is very small.

So you have to move in quickly and make things happen. That is how you win! We'll talk more about making the correct decisions in the chapter on Work Ethics.

You avoid negative energies by developing the positive energies we discussed: optimism, self-reliance, responsibility and being grateful. All these character traits should fill up your emotional tank with positive energy so there is no place for the negative energy. After this, just do your work, and be successful, be widely successful.

HE SENT HER TO OUTER-SPACE!

Did you ever see a millionaire living in a run down suburb with a lot of crime and insecurity? Not often, right?

In the same way, have you ever seen a poor person hanging out in very wealthy neighbourhoods? Not very likely again.

You might say it costs too much, but going to the beach in that expensive neighbourhood or a local café or to a golf course may not cost much. Yet poverty and negativity stick together. They say birds of a feather flock together. Meaning the environment is everything. We are affected by our family, our upbringing whilst we're young. It affects our vocabulary by way of association. If a young person is brought up in a neighbourhood where success means selling drugs, then it's likely that is what success will mean for them. If success means going to space and being a top neurosurgeon then it's very likely that child will pursue those things. Environment is everything.

For Azim Rizvee, an entrepreneur in real estate, changing environment meant sending his only daughter Zainab to space. She is only 12 years old and already wears the hijab. She is regularly attending training to prepare for the trip to outer space that the Virgin Galactic company organizes. The father Azim wants his daughter to see the Earth from that angle and start thinking big, without limitations. I could tell from our encounters that Zainab is already a big dreamer like her father.

This takes us back to choosing who to hang out with. We will discuss this more on the chapter of The Power of The Group. To develop positive thinking you must surround yourself with positive people.

What I've seen in other successful people is that they are very careful about their friends. They will have friends that are righteous that remind them of the next life. And they also have friends that help them in furthering their goals. They have friends that are uplifting.

They may not all be rich, but they have to be uplifting and not tear down their dreams. This is very fundamental on your journey to success.

3

CHANGE FOR THE BETTER

CHANGE IS NECESSARY

Now that we've talked about the Muslim character and its traits, it would be useless to continue further if we cannot change. Can we really change? Can our personalities change? Are we born the way we are today?

That's one of the key things I learnt from successful entrepreneurs. They are always growing and always learning. No one is born a leader. Again, entrepreneurs are not born they are developed. How else do you go from running a small pizza shop like the Mirza brothers to owning a multi-million dollar empire with businesses spanning the globe and employing thousands of people and impacting many lives? How do you go from humble beginnings to multimillion-dollar success?

How do you go from being a bus driver, with minimal access to the English language, like Sir Anwar Pervez, to being the chairman of Bestway UK, with billionaire status?

It all comes down to change. Change is good. Change is necessary. The world is changing. How did these Muslim entrepreneurs change?

Well, first of all, in order to change you have to be open to receive the guidance of other people. You have to see the opportunity and do something that you're not used to doing. You also have to be willing to do what someone else tells you to do.

Many business leaders I talked to had mentors. Some, if they came from business families, had their parents or older siblings as their mentors. Or they would find someone else that had the results to guide them. It could be from courses or long distance mentors. Whatever it was, they were still learning and were constantly developing.

You also have to develop the attitude of saying, 'it is possible! It is possible for me to change'. I went to Florida recently with my wife, and in Orlando there is a world famous zoo. In that zoo there is a polar bear that was playing with a ball.

The bear was walking on two legs and was juggling the ball with its nose like a pro soccer player. Now think about it: if a polar bear can play with a ball with just its nose... Even more amazingly, it has been trained to ride a small bicycle! So if a polar bear can change so much to accomplish that, then think about what is possible for you, a human being? Know that it's possible. It's a matter of will. You can really change a lot and get the results that you want.

THE RICHEST MAN IN AFRICA

Patience is really the most important trait of all the good character we see in the Quran. Impatience is and has always been the gateway to sin. Patience gives you as an entrepreneur the backbone that separates the successful from the failures. If you have patience, you will keep going where others have given up. Study any successful person and you will see their patience in the background. This leads to perseverance and success.

Many Muslim Entrepreneurs possess this character trait on a deep level. Take someone like Mr. Sulaiman Al Rajhi of Saudi Arabia. He grew up very poor, started doing odd jobs at a young age and amassed enough capital to open a money exchange business. He eventually founded the al-Rajhi islamic bank which became the largest bank in the country.

Or take someone like Dr. Yaqub Mirza who started his company back in the 1980s yet is still running it to this day. You can't run a company for that long without patience. It is only in the last decade that he saw exponential growth in his enterprise.

Mr. Aliko Dangote of Nigeria, the biggest entrepreneur in the African continent at this time had a similar journey. It took him over two decades to accumulate his first billion dollar but only a few years later his fortune ballooned to over $20 billion.

Why am I telling you this? Because without these character traits, you won't see the results you want.

As an entrepreneur you are just planting seeds in one season and you have to wait for the harvest. The harvest may come six months or a year from now. Sometimes it may take five years. In the Quran, the word for success that Allah uses is *aflaha*, which means success after a long period of time. *Aflaha* literally means a harvest that has been reaped by a farmer after a long wait.

You see: the farmer doesn't say "Hey I'm going to plant," and tomorrow he asks, "Where is the harvest?" The farmer takes care of the seed, plants it, tills the soil, waters it, takes care of pests and weeds, takes care of the produce and gets the return in some cases after years. In the case of coffee, you reap three years after planting.

It's the same with your enterprise; you must have a long term vision. Sometimes, it will take years and years before you reach a big result. But here is the thing; it would be worth it.

THE NUMBER ONE BROKER

Among the positive emotions, humility has to really be the first positive emotion to cultivate. Humility is not a personality trait. It is recognizing that you don't have something. It's being open to learning. Just be open. Be open to ask for help from people that may have the answers.

Lets talk about you and your enterprise. Having the humble spirit is to ask people that have the results that you want to have.

People that have been interviewed in this book may have your answers. So look for what's driving them. What are their thinking processes? And ask for help. That's one of the things I've seen across the board from these successful people. They have a humble sprit and are always willing to learn.

From my discussions with Azim Rizvee, I learnt that he is always travelling and attending conferences on business and technology to push his enterprise into the 21st century. He is at a very high level of thinking. It's very interesting to see that no matter how much success he has, he is always pushing the boundary and always learning.

One day, he could be learning about space exploration and participate in preparing his daughter for the space flight. The next time, he may be learning about how to give people a seven star hospitality experience. He visited the world's only seven star hotel in Dubai to learn that.

Now he is applying those principles to give his customers a better experience for his real estate business. You can see the effects of this in the results he gets. He is always willing to learn and to ask for help.
When he ran for office, he asked for help from his community. He asked the Muslim community as well as the city at large.

Being humble is a key factor for your success in business and in life. So start asking for help. More things will be accomplished this way.

A 50 YEAR OLD YOUNG MAN

The Muslim attitude is the positive attitude. One of the components of a good attitude is optimism. If you want to succeed in your enterprise, develop the skill and emotion of optimism. In bad times, optimism is key.

No matter what's happening, even in the face of death, the Muslim is told to restrain his speech and speak positively. In times of war, hunger and disease, we practice optimism. Easier said than done, but once you master this, you will truly rise to very high levels of success both spiritually and in this temporal world.

One of the key elements that I see in Muslim entrepreneurs like Mujeeb Ur Rahman is to see the best in people in all situations. In the face of bankruptcy, jail and many things that went wrong he developed that positive and uplifting attitude of optimism. It's an unparalleled characteristic of very successful Muslim entrepreneurs. To this day, in his fifties, he looks like a young man! After all his trials and tribulations, he is very well presentable and looks great. He's always well dressed, and I can tell you this emotional optimism is very important on your way to success.

It has been said that along the road of success, you will encounter many setbacks, many difficulties. But you must develop the ability to smile away those difficulties and move forward. Make those obstacles and difficulties your special weapons for the future.

CONFIDENCE BOOSTER

This really ties back to having a good self-image. Self-image is how you view yourself. It's as if you have a mirror in front of you, and instead of seeing your face, you are seeing your personality. How do you view yourself? With respect to others and many other metrics. How happy you are, how confident- these are all parts of how you view your own self. If you view yourself as someone successful, then very soon you will be if you are not already. So everything ties back to how you view yourself.

The reason why I found that some population groups are not as successful as others is because they have a poor self-image full of doubt, worry and blame.

It's probably true that other people are partly responsible for the situation you are in, but is it helpful? Does it help you to cling to those emotions and facts? No! You don't want to drag yourself down. All you want is the positive that will lead you to the path of success. You can deal with injustices after you succeed.

Take the example of Mr. Sulaiman al-Rajhi who went from poverty to great wealth. He owns various factories and even the largest organic halal meat farm in the Middle East!

Once, a fire destroyed one of his biggest factories. The plant manager was very reluctant to tell him the bad news. Upon hearing abou the fire, his only reply was: "Alhamdulillah!"
Allah SWT is the Bestower of wealth and Mr. Sulaiman did not waste any time complaining about it.

Again, as someone that is looking to succeed, don't waste your time with negative things. It will just damage your self-confidence. Negative news, negative things happening to your people, constantly worrying about losing wealth, health, family- that will not help you get self-confidence. On the contrary, it will drag your self-confidence.
One of the quickest ways is to develop your self-confidence. Really believe in yourself. Believe you can do it; that you already have what is necessary to get it done.

This comes from competence, which is knowing how to do what you're doing. If you're riding a bicycle for the first time, it would be very difficult to feel confident. However, if you have done it many times and have been around town with the bicycle your confidence increases. Business is no different.

Now how do you increase your self-confidence? By saying what I call the self-confidence manifesto.

It's a formula, a key that will open the door to a life full of self-confidence. Tell yourself:
"I am happy and grateful today that I am a millionaire, I am a servant of people, I execute all my plans. I am so happy and grateful about myself, my relationship with my family and my connection with the Creator.

_____

GOALS

1

SET BIG GOALS

WHEN A MILLIONAIRE FEELS BROKE

You have to realize that your Creator loves excellence. You want to excel in whatever you do and reach the highest level.

"Allah is Excellent and loves excellence" is a saying of the prophet SAW.

You have to also consider the magnitude of who you are dealing with. What is gold, really? It's just metal to its Creator. He can create more. What is a few bricks to make a beautiful home?
What is a great career? Nothing much in the great scheme of things. So consider it that way, think of the magnitude of your Creator and you will be free.

My good friend Mr. Arif Mirza told me that people ask him, "Arif, why do you ask for so much?" He always says in reply:

"Because Allah is so much. He is so powerful. Why not ask for more?"

- Arif Mirza, Serial Entrepreneur

That is the mindset of the Muslim entrepreneur. He sees bigger. He wants to have more and do more for himself and the people around him.

You must expand your comfort zone to be more successful. You are where you are because this is where you're comfortable.

Wealthy people have told me "your comfort zone is your broke zone!" We are all broke at different income levels. What is rich really? It's all relative. You might be rich compared to someone that doesn't have drinking water or someone living in the desert. A millionaire may be rich in your eyes, but if he's hanging around billionaires, he will feel broke.

So if you want to make it to the top, you have to expand your comfort zone. Daily, there are things you can do to expand your comfort zone. The first thing is to set big goals. Ridiculous goals that make you uncomfortable and make you move forward. We will discuss this point later in the section 'The straight path to success' of the present chapter.

SHE MEANT BUSINESS

If you have the correct niyyah (intention), then you are ready to receive help. This may be divine help or help from business associates. Know why you are doing what you are doing and what is the contribution you want to bring to the market. You want to know your business, product and service. Is this the right time? Now when you're ready to go in, you go in with the right intention. You can change directions along the way, but you also want to know where you are going from the start.

This is what I've seen from the most successful entrepreneurs I've interviewed. For example, Mrs. Ameena Sayed, director of Oxford Press Pakistan, has been very successful because she knew from the get go that she wanted to be the editor in chief and publish books she liked as a career. After starting her own book distribution firm, she ended up working to establish a branch for a large international publishing company in Pakistan. This goes to show the apple doesn't fall far from the tree. Really, when you have the correct intention it is like a gyroscope that leads you to success. It gives you the proper focus in order to realize your goals and dreams.

CLEAR YOUR MIND

You want to clear your mind, absolutely! Nowadays with social media, YouTube, email etc. – it's very difficult to clear your mind in such a jungle of ideas and chaos. All successful people I interviewed had a clear mind.

How can you achieve any success if your ideas are not clear? You need to have a clear mind if you want to draw a plan or if you want to work on a difficult problem and get new ideas for your business. The same goes if you're trying to learn new skills or solve challenges you are encountering in your business. Even to write this book, I had to force myself to clear my mind. Nothing gets done without focus.

I was talking to an Islamic scholar the other day and he told me that in the old days, the sign of childhood was to be day dreaming all over the place and have ideas bouncing everywhere. That's childhood. Adulthood is the capacity to really have the reigns on your own thinking so you can focus on the task at hand.

You can use this focus power in your own enterprise.

You first need to form a mental picture of your vision for the future. Do you want to earn a certain amount of money? Do you want your business to do a certain revenue? Do you want your store to be a certain way? Do you want to have a certain kind of house?

Well, you need to form a specific mental picture of all of this in your mind. Then you need to see yourself winning. This is critical. It's one of the ingredients to success.

The second step is to see yourself with the good that you desire. Is that a beautiful home? Is that travelling somewhere? Is it a certain profession? Is it to become the best scholar in your profession? Is it meeting with people to enhance your business? You need to see yourself doing that action. That's how you realize it.

Look at children. They are always imitating the adults, and that is how they master new things every single day. I am always amazed to see my two-year old nephews speak three languages almost fluently. They are probably saying to themselves: " If everybody speaks, of course I can speak!" And they do!

Hopefully after meeting all these successful Muslim Entrepreneurs, you will say: " I can do it too."

Now the Muslim has an advantage here because he prays five times a day: it is in his routine. This really helps us to envision the next life and our goal for it over and over, and over again. It trains us to concentrate on the task at hand. So if you're already putting this into practice during your Salah, it should be no big deal to concentrate when you work.

THE STRAIGHT PATH TO SUCCESS

Today, you can just walk around and you'll see that most people have no idea why they are doing what they are doing. They become a wandering generality.

I recently met an old friend of mine who did an engineering degree at the Masters level. Let us call him Ibrahim for the sake of the example. I asked Ibrahim what he wanted to do later on in life. His plan was to work for a firm and start making some money. Now that is a noble goal but I realized it was lacking something. There was no focus. He did not know how long he was going to work and in what capacity. Many young men and women have the same issue. They have no idea about what they want to do.

Obviously the goal for the next life is to worship your Creator, but in this life, what are you suited for? What kind of legacy do you want to leave for future generations? What work or contribution will you leave behind?

Those are serious questions! If left unanswered, failure creeps in whether you are an entrepreneur or you are working for someone else. Today, two years after our encounter, Ibrahim is still working as a security guard and waiting to get his dream job. He just wanted to get by, to get the minimum and pay the bills, he got it. Be careful what you wish for. You might end up getting just that..

Your clear aspiration could be to become a teacher, if that is where you find satisfaction in life. It could be being an amazing mother that raises righteous Muslim children. It could be to become a millionaire. It could be anything; there are thousands and thousands of aims. That is the main problem. A lot of people just wander around, getting a job here and there, and at the end of their life they end up broke.

You don't want that to happen to you, so select a clear aspiration. Some authors have called it a definite chief aim or a definite purpose.
Select something you desire ardently in your heart of hearts, and pursue it. That's one of the most important things you can do for your success. In the earlier section on goal setting, we discussed how you want to visualize this aim every single day if not hourly. See it at least once a day. Put it in writing if possible, or have some pictures to remind you of your goal and clear purpose.

When you develop an ardent desire for wealth, the sky is the limit for you. Your mind is like a magnet. So if you hold a thought long enough in your mind, you will eventually start seeing opportunities around you. A recent example is when I spent an afternoon with one of my Muslim Entrepreneur mentors. He made notice that because I was driving a certain car, I was noticing that car everywhere. Even behind my back. Your goal is no different. If you see it all the time, you will notice opportunities that will allow you to accomplish it.

Your mind is acting as nothing more than the gyroscope that will point you to the right direction. The mind is a very powerful tool, and really it is the only tool we have complete control over.

Even in difficult situations, if you have your mind intact, you are in control. You can still think what you want to think and have the intention you want. That is real freedom. It's the only freedom our Creator gave every single one of us.

1% OF A BILLION

Your thinking got you exactly where you are right now. If your best thinking got you a result you dislike, then all you have to do is change your philosophy and get a different result. Get new thinking.

It might just be that you don't know what you don't know. I have failed at many ventures in the past, and I can tell you that before starting any of them, I was pretty confident they would work out. But along the way, I would always think "I should have listened to so-and-so who has more experience." This is true for every venture. If you're not achieving your goals right now, the reason is usually very simple. There are things you don't know, and if you knew them, success would be easier. In other words, if you think the way rich people think, then there is a big chance that you would succeed.

One of the discussions I had with Imam Ashraf Zaghloul, CEO of NTG Clarity Inc. was that many entrepreneurs are people with ideas that like to dream. When you're starting a new company, you may think your idea is so valuable that you have to keep it secret and protect it at all costs. But that's not how rich entrepreneurs think.

Usually, when Imam Ashraf goes into ventures, he finds the most competent people to run the business and get it successfully into the market. He looks for the shortest and most effective route possible. The unsuccessful entrepreneur is always thinking about protecting their idea, which is why their business doesn't grow.

One time, a wannabe entrepreneur approached him with a business idea. He wanted Imam Ashraf to partner with him. They were supposed to form a partnership but there was a problem. He wanted Imam Ashraf to invest not only his time and business experience but also his money. What does he get in return? A measly 5%! Needless to say he was not interested.

That person was not thinking the right way.

It's like owning 1% of a billion dollar company, which will still allow you to become a millionaire, or owning 100% of a company that is in debt. The imam told me, "you choose which one you want Oumar!" The choice is clear. This is new and high level thinking, these are things you most likely haven't heard before about forming partnerships. This is what you want to do in order to grow towards your dream.

2

THE POWER OF DU'A

WATCH WHAT YOU SAY

The word was given exclusively to the human being, he has the ability to speak. Allah says,

'He has created man. He has taught him speech.'

- Al-Quran, Surah Ar-Rahman, Ayah 3-4

Language was taught like revelation.

Now when you use your tongue to ask something of your Creator, something very powerful happens. The words we say have an effect on our lives and our environments. On the divine scale, Allah SWT says: "Be!" and it is.

In the same way, with the permission of Allah SWT, your tongue really attracts what you say to you. So if someone says: "I am sad, I am sad, I am sad", this person becomes sad. If someone is talking about how they are afraid of sickness, they become sick.

You will be amazed that most illnesses are not caused by germs but by the minds and tongues of the people. The same thing happens if a person talks about their fear of being poor or losing their job. When the tongue is not controlled, it brings all those negative things to the person. We sometimes do it mindlessly.

Now, here is a word of warning for the student of wealth: if you see your brother or sister blessed with wealth and success, say "MashaAllah"(Allah willed it). Someone has beautiful children and you want to praise them, say "MashaAllah". It instantly eliminates the evil that can come between two people like envy, jealousy etc.

THE MILLIONAIRE THAT PRAYS AT NIGHT

All of us have heard about the power of du'a or invocations in the Islamic religion. Your du'a is not just in your mind, you say it with your tongue.

It's just like creation, like using your own tongue for creating. But it only happens with the permission of Allah.
When someone gossips, we know it is literally eating someone's flesh. It really is physical, even if we don't see it.

In the same way in the positive realm, when we say:
"I am grateful, I am thankful to Allah, I am grateful for my parents, I will succeed, I am a winner."

Believe it or not, when you keep saying it again and again, the good things come to you. Really, dua is in part the repetition of those positive things and thanking God, of being thankful. So is the dhikr. When you say subhanAllah and Alhamdulillah, you are continuously praising and thanking Allah over and over again. You are then in a state of gratitude, which allows you to receive more. So, keep saying what you desire. Keep telling yourself you are a millionaire if this is your goal, keep saying, "I'm so happy and grateful to Allah that I'm a millionaire" over and over again. This will put you in a positive frame of mind to work and win as an entrepreneur.

Arif Mirza, the internet entrepreneur and investor based in Dubai puts it this way: "I wake up for tahajjud every day. I don't ask any man, woman or king for any help, I ask Allah to give me everything and the reason I wake up for tahajjud is because that's when Allah comes down and He looks for people and I want to be one of those people I want to say Allah I'm here give me." Ask and you will receive!

THE AMAZING CONDITION

The law of attraction is a term used by many modern business thinkers. It says we attract what we are. If you have an attractive personality and think good things, you will attract good.

And if you have bad thinking you will attract bad. Attractive thoughts attract attractive people and attractive opportunities.

Some go as far as to say that we can create our futures through our tongues. But can we find any evidence of this 'law' in the Islamic tradition and is it being used by the Muslim entrepreneurs?

The first point is that if we expect good from Allah, then we will get it. Allah will come to you with good. If you expect bad, Allah will give you bad. This is in our tradition though it hasn't been called the law of attraction. We believe everything is from Allah, to whom we all return.

The second point is a word of caution against the predominant law of attraction users. Some western philosophers suggest that we literally create our destiny with our strong will. We become co-creators with God. They have reported great results with this approach. However this is the essence of magic and is unlawful in the Islamic perspective. Only Allah creates the future. This book is not a theological book so I will not go further with this analysis.

Now, how do you use this law of attraction? Just like we mentioned before, by developing a positive attitude.
You want to control your thoughts, and only think about what you want to happen. This is the positive, it will attract positive things to you. So ask yourself, will I be willing to talk about my thinking? Will I be willing to broadcast my thoughts in public because they are so uplifting? If the answer is no, then you need to stop immediately and replace them with positive and uplifting thoughts.

You can speed up this process by asking refuge from the whisperings of the devil (shaitan).

Most of us, if we make a mistake or get rejected tend to beat ourselves down and tell ourselves we're worthless or things of that sort. If we said those things to anybody else, we wouldn't have any friends! It would be highly insulting to say these things to others. But we are so harsh on our own selves! And what I'm telling you to do is to be easy on yourself.

Some of you have businesses, and if you're not succeeding right now it's OK! Everything is fine. Everything will be fine. It's all OK. I know you will win. You are a winner. You've already won. And that's the spirit of the Muslim, as Sheikh Hamza Yusuf reminded me, the Quran says, "the Muslims have already succeeded!" If you think the right way then truly you will meet the right people, get the right opportunities – and that is all from Allah.

However, I do not suggest that bad things won't happen. They will. In droves. Those can be a good in disguise. As the prophet SAW said:

"Amazing is the condition of the believer, when good happens he rejoices, and when bad happens, he thanks Allah and is patient. In both cases he is rewarded."

We do not create the results ourselves. It all comes from Allah. All we can do is have that positive attitude so that we are open to receive positive things.

3

CONCEIVE THEN ACHIEVE

LIFT THAT CAR !

Without a why, you won't do anything. Your why is very important for you as an entrepreneur. If you are someone who is committed to win, you need to have the proper mindset. If you don't know why you're doing what you're doing, then it won't be attractive long enough for you to keep going and be able to win.An entrepreneur without a strong why is just going to give up and get a job.

We talked about setting your goals and hopefully you did so already. Now what you want to add to your goal is the emotion.
You have to have a certain amount of emotion attached to your goal in order to do it, otherwise it will be just knowledge. Knowledge is just information. It does not move anybody. What you want is applied knowledge. What will make you move is that emotion; that 'why'.

Once you have a why, the how is taken care of. Let's say you want to start an internet business, if you know why you want to do it, and you're emotional about it, you'll know how to do it.

You'll spend days and nights to figure out the techniques and all the how-to s you need to know in order to win.

There was once a lady whose son got trapped by a small car. She was so emotional about it that she lifted the car up with her bare arms. The son was rescued. Now, she didn't need to get a manual on how to bench press and get muscles to lift a car. She just did it in the heat of the moment, because she had a big why. Her pride and joy, that boy was trapped by the car. A day after the incident, there is no way she could lift the car, because the why isn't there anymore. This example shows you why you need something to drive you to take action.

Find out what your why is. Is it your family? Is it because you want to be free? I had a conversation about this with Dr. Faruk El Baz, the famous Egyptian scientist that worked on the Apollo program. His why was his two daughters. He had to put bread on the table. This enabled him to work the extra long hours he needed to secure his position on the Apollo 16 program, the first mission to the moon. What is it for you?

FROM BASEMENT TO MANSION

The word desire has sometimes got negative connotations. It is true that Allah compares the one with desire for dunya to a slave, also to a dog that has his tongue forever lulling out; not a very attractive image. I will show you how important it is for you as an entrepreneur to have the right kind of desire, that will free you of the negative desires that chain us to this life.

Without desire, you won't have the emotion necessary to keep going. Nobody said this journey would be easy, but that desire inside of you will allow you to achieve your goal. Desire will make you go to work. Desire will allow you to stay up at night to work on your dreams and on your goals, to learn new skills and sharpen your axe. Everything then becomes effortless after a while.

Mr. Muhammad Salim Siddiqi, a successful accountant with his own business, had a big desire to be successful after losing his job at a firm following eighteen years of loyal service. This happens to a lot of people after companies downsize. It's the sad instability of the employment world. Yet, Salim had a desire to take care of his family, even though he had no money and was broke.

He and his wife decided to restart their business in his basement, an accounting business. They waited patiently until they got their first client. When they did, they were overjoyed to get their first phone call.

Now it's all history. He lives in a voluptuous mansion. He has the opportunity to inspire other aspiring entrepreneurs to keep going.

So get a strong desire to win. It's necessary to push you. When you have that desire, you will have no problem getting the idea in your head and hold it long enough for you to accomplish it. You want to have that desire in order to accomplish your goal.

Most of the successful people I see have been in their respective line of businesses for ten, fifteen or twenty years without changing, because they love it and are passionate about it. They know close to everything about it and are experts on it.

If you don't really love it, you will tend to jump around and change lines of business. That's not the smart way to become successful. Choose one line of business and find the people succeeding in that line of business. That's the way to make it to the top.

HOW A HORSE GOT ME THERE

All the successful people I have seen have a goal in mind. It will allow you to go to your destination. You start from point A to go to point B and that goal will allow you to do that. Then you need to write it down. This allows you to memorise that goal and to have it intuitively in your mind. When you write it down, it gives you that commitment. Commit it to memory. Then have it where you can see it every single day. See your goal.

This reminds me of when I was sitting an exam in France for the best engineering school. I had the goal and wanted it so badly that I drew a picture of me riding a horse.

On that drawing were written the words: 'Go For it!". I had it on my desk, and I could see it every single day when I sat down to do maths. The same goes for you.

If you really want it, if you really desire that which you say, then it will be intuitive for you to go for it. I did it without reading a single book on goal setting. It was a natural thing to do. It's what all successful people do. Now you need to be specific. Don't say "I want a lot of money". Say exactly how much! Say "I want to make $100,000", or $500,000, or $1 million or even $10 million. Then put a deadline on it, one year, five years- it can be a short or long-term range.

Make it reasonable, otherwise you won't believe your goal and it will be useless. Then the final step is a little bit less intuitive; it is to have something in it for you. What will you give yourself once you accomplish the goal? That will allow you to be motivated to get it done.

Someone involved in humanitarian causes may say to themselves that they want to raise $10 million for a certain country or neighbourhood. Suppose that person says : "If I get 10 million dollars, I will give it all in charity and help orphans etc." Do you really believe he will accomplish that goal? It is very unlikely. He will just say: "well, at least, I tried". There is no emotion behind it and nothing to gain. Remember this:

"There is a difference between a goal and a wish."

Have something to lose for not hitting your goal and reward yourself if you reach it. Otherwise, it will be very difficult for you to accomplish it because you won't be looking forward to getting there.

Give something to yourself. It could be a cake, it could be travel, it could be a weekend away with your spouse or a better car. Have something there for you and watch what will happen.

When I was young, the goal was to get the best grade in class especially in math and physics.

Every time I had over 17 out of 20, my dad would give me money. This was always exciting for me and my performance went through the roof! The same applies for you as a Muslim Entrepreneur. Reward yourself for reaching a key milestone.

SO WHAT'S THE PLAN?

On your journey to success, now that you have a dream and a goal and a strong desire, you need a plan to go through with it. Now you are committed. You're almost there. All that is left is a plan that will allow you to go from where you are to where you want to be.

From my interviews, I've seen that most successful entrepreneurs want to go the shortest route possible. Sometimes that route can be achieved by asking the right question to the right kind of people. Ask the right questions. Then devise the right plan of action. Because you don't want to commit to someone else's plan. You know yourself. You know your capabilities. You know what you can do.

And as one philosopher said: "all you can do is all you can do, and all you can do is enough."

Now, make this plan reasonable. Make a note of what you will do every day. But don't make it too stressful on you. Yours may be to work eight hours a day. It may be to call two people a day.

It may be to collect a bit of money, save it to invest and start your own business. Whatever it may be, make it reasonable so that you believe you can reach it. And then work the plan. Yes there is work involved!

How much work is required and which price you have to pay for success will be examined in the chapter of Work Ethics.

The last step to your plan of action is making it incremental. Say, next month you want to be earning this much.

There is a myth going on in our modern times that you can reach success instantaneously. That's why lottery is so popular nowadays! Well you can manufacture your own (halal) lottery by making your earning incremental. Say I want to earn a $1,000,000 in three years. Or I may say in six months I have a goal to earn $5,000 or $10,000 a month. Make it incremental, make it believable. Once you reach it, proceed further with your plan of action.

THE SHORTEST ROUTE

Motivation is like taking a shower; it just doesn't last too long before you need it again. But commitment is what turns dreams and goals into reality.

If you are committed, then you know that you are not going to quit when times get rough. And times will get rough!

Imam Ashraf Zaghloul, founder of NTG Clarity told me that in his business at one point he wasn't able to pay the payroll. But he kept the dream alive. He believed. He did du'a. And he made a lot of istighfar (you ask forgiveness for your sins) because that increases your wealth.
And the money 'magically' appeared.
He was committed to make it work. He didn't say, 'let me go find a job', or 'let me leave this project and start another one'. He stuck it out and got it done. Success follows certain principles; it is not a product of magic or luck. As Holton Buggs said:

"Commitment to continuity brings with it emotional stability."

You have to commit to keep going, you have to commit to the daily actions and disciplines that will lead you to success. If you do it you will be very emotionally stable because the result won't matter. All that matters is the process. You are happy because you are doing what you know you're supposed to be doing. If you don't do that then you will become very emotionally unstable, leading to being sad or soar in your own self.

As the poem said: "if you're committed to continuity and there is no turning back, then you must go forward. And if you must go forward, then losing is not an option. And if losing is not an option, success becomes inevitable."
So keep going! Success is inevitable.

ASK THOSE WHO KNOW

You want to identify the right people to work with. Those people will help you accomplish your goal and desire. Everything you want in life has been placed in someone else's hands as you move along.

As a child, you needed your parents. As a student, you needed your teachers. So it's amazing to see that in the business world, many people are not willing to go and seek out help. There is nothing wrong with asking for help. You will always need it from others, and in return, you help others by bringing your expertise to the market place.

So go out and seek out the people that will allow you to accomplish your dream and your goal. One of the things I learnt from successful Muslim Entrepreneurs is that they make du'a for Allah to place the right people on their path.

That's an affirmation for you right there. Ask for the right people to appear. Ask for the right opportunity and the right timing, and see what happens.

4 x YOUR FAILURE RATE

In order for you to reach your goals, what you want to do is begin the journey with the end in mind.

Think of that picture of your goal and know where you're going.

Once you have that end in mind, work your plan while keeping the end in mind. Sooner or later, you'll reach it. If you fail, failure is just temporary. Let us say the goal is you'll be earning x amount in one year. And one year comes but you don't reach it. Then it's no big deal. All you have to do is reset that goal. Reset that date. If the date of completion is passed and you did not reach your goal, reset the date and start over! You're your own boss. You don't have to fire yourself. Make adjustments. Victory usually comes an inch after the place where you almost gave up.

The other way to hit your goal faster is for you to avoid doing the minimum. You see, avoid being a minimalist. So if you have to call 5 people to get one sale, call 10. Call 20! Don't be a minimalist. You don't have to make your minimum your maximum.

HAVE I ARRIVED?

This is a big question. Now that you hit that proverbial one million, what to do next? Do you just give up and be a couch potato? I can tell you this happens to a lot of Olympic athletes whose only goal was to get the gold medal! You got it, so what?

You see, in order for you to keep performing, you must have the habit of resetting your goal. You reached it, fine celebrate! Then reset. Was it one million? Now make it ten, make it twenty. You helped 5000 people reach financial freedom, but are you employing 10,000? Like Mr. Shahzad Asghar who is running his own textile mills in Pakistan. He is responsible for 10,000 pay cheques. That's a fantastic accomplishment!

Are you helping a hundred people right now? Set it higher, make it a thousand! Do you earn ten million? Make it a billion! Why not? The bounties of Allah are infinite.

NASA found that many of their retired astronauts were becoming couch potatoes. Once they went to space and accomplished their dream, there was no life left in them. Some of them ended up in depression or committing crimes because they had no other goal.
They started teaching their astronauts how to reset goals and aim higher. Be better every time. The problem was solved.

Ever met one of those high school geniuses that get the best marks? Many of them don't succeed in the business world if they have no set goals and dreams. Success is not an event. It's a process to be enjoyed. Once you reach what you thought was success, be grateful, then set it higher. That will keep you going.

A Muslim is someone that is always striving for a higher level. Jannatul Firdaus is the highest point to aim for in Jannah. The prophet SAW said if you ask for jannah ask for jannatul firdaus. Don't be a minimalist! Go higher, aim higher. Reset your goals.

And once you achieve a milestone, celebrate! Make yourself happy for getting that goal. Don't downsize it and say it's nothing, celebrate! And make it known to people, make known what Allah blessed you with. Are you prosperous in your business? Celebrate it with your family. Buy your wife something! Enjoy your new bounties, and watch what will happen to your bank account.

PRINCIPLE V

BELIEF

1

BELIEF SYSTEM OF SUCCESS

UNWAVERING

What is real belief? This is really one of my favourite chapters, if not my most favourite. Belief!

Through my conversations with some of the most successful Muslim Entrepreneurs, I came across reverts. Many have interesting journeys. What you will find is that their belief was born sometimes through a dream, like in the case of Dr. Amina Coxon. Then, they opened the Quran, and it starts:

"This is the Book about which there is no doubt..."

-Al-Quran, Surah Al-Baqarah, Ayah 2

How many books do you know that start that way? Declaring there is no doubt in it.

What does that tell you?

First of all, it tells you that you have to believe. With full conviction. It's not a wavering belief. It's not a "maybe" belief. It is a belief without a doubt. That's the belief we want.

Now you want to adopt the same philosophy in your business. If you are wavering right now, if you don't believe right now, do you really think people will believe in you, if you don't believe in yourself? So, the first step is to grow your belief. Grow and extend your belief.
The second point is the belief in Islam is a belief that is not superstitious. It is a belief founded in proof and evidence. In the same way, that is what you want your business to be.

THE AYAH OF SUCCESS

This is really the culmination of the Muslim Entrepreneur's mindset. We talked about setting goals, we talked about how to plan and follow through to reach higher and higher levels. Now what I want to tell you is how to really reach your goal and your dream by using the Quran.

This tip comes from my friend and mentor of many, Imam Ashraf, founder of NTG Clarity Networks Inc. He likes to call it the ayat of success.

The preceding ayat says :

"Whoever should desire the immediate - We hasten for him from it what We will to whom We intend…"

-Al-Quran, Surah Al-Israh, Ayah 18

And then the ayah of success says:

"But whoever desires the Hereafter and exerts the effort due to it while he is a believer - it is those whose effort is ever appreciated."

-Al-Quran, Surah Al-Israh, Ayah 19

You have to have a desire to achieve something and believe that you will reach it which is what we talked about. Believing makes you special. Everything is based on belief. For the Muslim, it is our belief in Allah.

It will also apply to non-Muslims as long as they believe in themselves and their goal and enterprise or product. As a salesman, you want to believe in your service to reach that high level of success. As a Muslim, you believe in Allah and that you will get success through the abilities He has given you. Through this belief, we know that the One that is able to give without counting can give to you as well. This is the ayah of success. Follow it and see how you prosper.

The ayah of success from Surah Israh sums up what success is.
It starts with belief. It's about action following that belief.

So, you have to grow your belief as quickly as possible. Don't take too long to believe, just believe and roll with belief.

People will invest in your business, product and even on yourself if you believe.

Salim Siddiqi started his business in a basement, late in life. Yet he had the belief that he wanted to be his own boss. He knew it was possible. And he started his business. No backing, no large sums of money, he didn't make any excuses. He just believed that he would be successful.

That is why this ayah starts with belief; it's the most precious commodity out there. We discussed this when we talked about self image; to increase your belief in yourself and in Allah. It's all about belief. Nothing will be accomplished without belief.

So, if right now you're running your business and you don't have any belief, change that. Realize that activity without belief is just exercise. You're just running through the motions. But when you have belief it will multiply everything that you do. It's contagious! People can sense belief. People can sense disbelief. People can sense belief just like a woman can sense love; miles away. If you want to win, make your belief so big that people, at worse, will think, "I don't think you'll accomplish this goal, but … you're crazy…" Even if they don't follow you! Eventually, someone will believe in you; because that's how belief works. It really is contagious.

THE MONEY SHOWED UP

As a Muslim Entrepreneur, the foremost difference between you and everyone else is really that belief in Allah. It manifests itself partly by complete reliance on Allah.

When you look at a bird; it goes out in the morning. The bird does not know whether or not it will eat. The bird knows that when it goes out, it will come back at night with a full stomach, as well as feed its family. Now do you have that life? Are you as certain of your rizq? Are you as certain of your pay cheque?

Most people are working a job nowadays. The reason why is because of certainty. They're certain of having a paycheque at the end of the month, like the bird is certain of getting fed. It is because they are more certain about the company paying them than about their own ability to generate the money.

You see, as a Muslim Entrepreneur, you have to be certain of your rizq through your enterprise. As certain as the other guy is of receiving his pay cheque. And that is the fundamental difference.

Another example I've seen of reliance is when my mentor Imam Ashraf Zaghloul founder of NTG Clarity Networks Inc. couldn't pay his payroll. The money wasn't there. But his reliance was. He said, "Nobody is willing to lend, and I can't pay the payroll." Yet he had reliance. His solution was to say a lot of Istighfaar.

He told everyone in his office to make a lot of Istighfaar (saying Astaghfirullah)

"Rely on Allah and make Istighfar."

-Ashraf Zaghloul, founder of NTG Clarity Networks Inc.

That included his accountant. Within a few days, the money showed up! Expect good things from Allah, and you will see good results. You see, you have to have that reliance that no one can benefit you, except Allah SWT. So when you do your actions as an entrepreneur, remember that.

Mujeeb Ur Rahman told me that there were tough times in his business, his family being threatened and so on. Whilst in jail, none of his friends or contacts showed up to help him. It was there that he realized only Allah can benefit him. You see, you have to make contacts with people, but you have to have the right intention. They cannot benefit you. They cannot harm you either. Unless Allah wills.

"I AM THE GREATEST"

Action without belief is just exercise.

We talked about belief and how to use it while working. Fear is really just an appearance. Reality is different. So do it despite of the fear. Do it, in spite of the uncertainty. Do it anyway. Set yourself up with enthusiasm for your enterprise.

You also have to stop speaking negatively about yourself. Speak positively and inevitably your belief will grow.

The first famous "Muhammad" in America is without a doubt the legendary boxer Muhammad Ali, an African American who embraced the Islamic faith. During the 60s up to the early 80s, he was the top boxer in the world. It was 1964, and the young Ali was up against the world champion of the time Sonny Liston. He made a speech that made him famous; "I am the greatest." Being the greatest, there is no way that Ali would lose. You can use the same power for your business.

YOU ARE A WINNER

You're reading this book because you want to be rich, to change your life, to know how to become a successful Muslim Entrepreneur, someone that has an impact all over the world. You want to change your family life. You want to change your nation's course. You want to enjoy the good life. Whatever your end goal is, you want to go in the direction of massive success. So how do you shift paradigms?

You see, in order to be rich you have to feel rich already. If you think like a poor person, if you behave like a poor person, then you will simply stay that person.

You have to view yourself, see yourself as already rich. That is the only way you'll become rich.

The size of your bank account doesn't have to dictate how you feel about yourself. Do you value yourself? Do you value your ideas? That has nothing to do with your bank account.

Say to yourself, "I'm rich!" "I'm a winner!" Yes, you are a winner.

Allah says in the Quran; He created man from semen. Science has discovered there are millions of cells in that semen, and one of them, that's you, ended up getting to that egg (your mother's).

What does that tell you? It tells you: of all the possible combinations, Allah chose you. Allah created you as the winning combination. Allah says, "He has honored the son of Adam". The angels were told to prostrate to our father, Adam.

So you are already a winner. Change your paradigm. Stop thinking thoughts like, "we are a defeated nation." "My country is poor." There is no defeated nation. There is no country that is poor. The only people that prosper are the people that feel good about themselves. When was the last time you heard a Chinese person say "my country is poor"?

You're not poor. You're a winner! That is the attitude you should have.

Another thing you must do is stop listening to negative things. Stop watching the news. Stop watching the suffering of the people. Be positive. Rely on Allah and know that you are a winning nation.
We are a nation that is leading. You are a winner. You have already won. Have you ever heard classification terms such as G-8, G-7, G-20?

Second world, third world, industrialised nations? All of these terms are subversive terms you don't want to use in your vocabulary. If you view yourself to be in a third world category, that is where you will stay. Have you noticed that countries rarely move from third world status to first world? That's how it's supposed to work. It's programming.

Yet it isn't true. You can get rich wherever you are right now. There is no need to move. There is no need to change countries or cities. Just change yourself. Find the rich people already in your country, in your neighbourhood. Change your circle and it will shift your paradigm.

2

NEGATIVE BELIEFS

HIJABI IN HOLLYWOOD

A baby is born with just two fears, the fear of loud noises and the fear of falling. Those are their only natural fears. There is also a natural fear of Allah.

That is what Islam calls the fitra, the natural disposition of a human being.

Everything else apart from that comes from unnatural limitations. Very often, we put unnatural limitations on ourselves. Most limitations come from our environment.

For example, it could be parents that say to their child, 'you can't do this!' or a person tries something and fails. In both cases, limitations can start to creep in. If you believe you're not eloquent, then you won't be eloquent. If you believe something is true about yourself it will be true.

Society has many established unnatural limiting beliefs. One of them could be that a Muslim woman is at a disadvantage. Yet in Islamic history, we know Khadijah RA was a wealthy businesswoman.
She didn't go out there and make things happen alone; she was intelligent enough to recruit and delegate good managers. She was an entrepreneur and a wise investor managing her assets.

That's how she married the prophet (SAW) who was one of her top managers. She recognised his good character. So Islam doesn't limit the woman in entrepreneurship; it will just give guidelines to how they should interact and do business. A woman could be extremely wealthy, and they certainly are in the Islamic world.

Lena Khan is a Muslim woman that wears the head scarf in Los Angeles, California. She does not think anything of limitations. She is the first Muslim director in Hollywood and is on her way to make big movie productions.

Race is another big one. There is no concept of race in Islam; there are only tribes, which the prophet (SAW) worked to unite.

Race is a Western concept. A lot of people claim to be from this continent or that race, and then expect to perform to a certain degree because of the limitations of their race. They may also limit themselves based on the accepted biases and assumptions about their religion or social origin.

In Islam, no matter what your religion was in the past, as long as you reform yourself and do your best to leave negative habits, everything else doesn't matter. There is no barrier between class or race. People pray together and are equal in the sight of God. Only human beings place these unnatural limitations, for example when saying 'I will only marry into one kind of people'.

There is also no such distinction between the poor and the rich.
Muslims should know that from the moment we're born, Allah has given us a special status and honour. Regardless of your social origin, you are very precious.

RICH MALAYSIA

Negative beliefs rob you of your most valued treasure: your belief. Imagine you became wealthy and decided to buy gold bars. You place your bars in your private coffer, that has a very secure lock.

Would you give the combination key to anybody or would you guard it preciously? Your mind is even more important.

A negative belief is a belief that really doesn't serve you. It's kind of like going on a hike. You don't want to do that with a heavy bag. If you're going to walk 10 miles with a big bag full of stones, things you don't need, it's kind of ridiculous! It's the same with people that hold onto past beliefs that don't serve them.

They think "I can't because it didn't work before."

You see, when you hold onto a negative belief from the past, you've just interpreted reality the wrong way. Let's say you tried something before and it didn't work. That just means you need to try something different! That's why Muslim Entrepreneurs are successful.
It's so much about having the right belief in yourself.

When Azim Rizvee told me that he wants to expand his daughter's belief in herself, that was very inspiring. You just have to hear him talk about space exploration and how he is planning to send his 12 years old to space. That's very exciting! You realize, wow, it is possible to do more. To be more. Especially for our children.

Another negative belief is to think "my country or my people are poor." If you believe that, in your mind, it will stay that way. The Japanese lost badly after World War II. Yet they never thought themselves poor. Malaysians refer to their country as "Rich Malaysia"! So never believe your country to be poor. You'd only be setting yourself up for failure. If you believe you can, you truly can.

Some of the very successful Muslim Entrepreneurs have a good image for their countries, even if they don't come from typically wealthy backgrounds. They started their enterprise and thought they could make their countries cleaner, more efficient, more pleasant, to gain international recognition.

So I want you to let go of the past. Make room for the future. A future where you are a winner. I do not mean by that that you ignore the poor people and pretend they do not exist. Rather focus on the riches of this world and you can serve the poor better once you become wealthy yourself.

THERE'S ENOUGH OUT THERE

You need belief that serves you. Discover the beliefs that are holding you back. Beliefs like supplies are limited. Very often in school they teach that concept. But the truth is there are enough riches in this world. They tell us the earth is over populated. This is not an Islamic belief. When Allah created us, He gave us ample supply. There is no mention of limited supply.

There is enough space in Australia alone for every single human being on earth to live comfortably with a garden and a house! So the Earth is more than big enough. The supply is large enough. There are mountains, there are oceans- all unexplored.

Now what are other beliefs that don't serve you? If you're from a Muslim country, you may be led to believe your country is a "third world" country.

This is not a belief that serves you. If you believe that you come from a "poor" country, this is not a belief that serves you.

A belief that serves you is that you are rich, that you can succeed, that you can win.

Discard all the beliefs that don't serve you.

If you believe that the world is unfair to you because of your colour, your gender, your religion, then these beliefs do not serve you. It could be true. But it could be untrue too.
Either way, it doesn't serve you. So don't use it. Use only the beliefs that serve you to create wealth, success and prosperity.

I will end with a word of advice for my brothers and sisters that are suffering the ills of racism and prejudice: the successful entrepreneurs are not blind to those ugly realities. They just choose not to focus on those. There is no better revenge than success. So focus all your energy on winning instead of complaining.

SHE KNEW HER STUFF

Really, the difference between belief and faith is that belief is based on proof. Belief is really faith, but with proof, based on something that we see. Faith is to believe in something and believe that it will happen.
As a Muslim Entrepreneur you start with faith. You launch and have the faith it will succeed.

You don't know the future, so you have faith. And as you start getting one sale, two sales… belief grows.

One of the lessons I learnt from Turkish architect Mrs. Selva Gurdogan is that it is important to know your business inside out in order to support your belief. She studied at some of the best architectural schools and she is today leading the world in certain aspects of urban planning. One of her famous projects was to design a space in Istanbul for bicycles. Another one was to find a way to manage the parking of more than 2.5 million cars in the mega-city.

With belief in your own abilities, there is no stopping the Muslim to reach a high standard of excellence.

Either you have 100% faith, or you have fear. You cannot have just 99% faith. As an entrepreneur that's working towards vision, you have to have total faith.

EITHER DOUBT OR HAVE FAITH

When you start your business, the first few years are typically the most difficult. You have to take your enterprise off the ground. There are no results yet. There is no belief yet. So what can you possibly base your belief on?

You just have faith in your future vision. If you're not careful, doubts can creep in. That's devastating to any business.

What you have to know is that doubts come from your environment. People you associate with. They also come from inappropriate preparation. So you started your business without preparing yourself. Mastery isn't necessary, but you have to at least start the process. If you're not prepared, doubts and distractions come easily. When doubts come in, they can hold tremendous consequences.

Sh. Saeed Rageah became an imam because someone told him, "I know you will become an imam." That's the power of people having faith in you! Even though at the time he wasn't planning to become one at all; he was studying to become a doctor! But once he got on that pulpit (minbar), people knew he was the real deal. Today he is a world famous imam and an entrepreneur that has a TV channel and motivates the youth to achieve more. What if he listened to the doubters who were frowning when he started his very first sermon. Thousands of people would not have been affected positively.

Doubts can also come in when you face failure after failure. But all those failures are just steps to your next success.

Mujeeb Ur Rahman started business with his brother in Doha. They would go on site and talk to people, get clients, drive to each building site they saw. At the end of five years in this way, they had a huge list of clients. But they were prepared. You have to be prepared. There is no place for doubts.

You can hear it in the voice of these entrepreneurs. Mr. Mujeeb told me every Muslim should be an entrepreneur! And they should believe without a doubt they will be successful.

Doubt is an indecisive habit. All the successful people I talked to are very decisive. When they make a decision, they stick to it. That's why they are where they are. So do yourself a favour. Eliminate indecisiveness. Be decisive. Be prepared for success. And then be decisive once you've prepared. Know you've taken the right steps. You have the right idea. And go with it without doubting.

3

GROW YOUR BELIEF

BUILD ON ROCK

Once you start your enterprise, you believe it is possible to succeed. Your optimism is at an all time high. But obstacles may pop up.

Sometimes people lie. Sometimes you lose a client. That has been true for every single successful entrepreneur that I've met; every single one of them! Obstacles tend to pop up.

So how do you maintain unwavering belief through those obstacles? How do you get a rock solid belief that nothing can shake?

First of all, have resolve. Resolve is, "I'm going to make this happen." A gentleman I met once said: "I'm going to be successful or die."

That's an immense amount of resolve! That gentleman came from a warzone, they lost all their possessions while migrating. Yet when he started his business, he still had the strength to say, "I'm going to become successful or die." Hopefully, a few rejections and failures won't make us die. So develop resolve!

Secondly, to grow your belief, you've got to be in motion all the time. All the time! Often times you start your business and obstacles pop up. So how do you grow that belief? Maybe you just had an argument with your wife about money because finances aren't great. You have to be in motion. You have to be in activity. You could even just go for a walk around the block; and you'll see that your mood will change. Do something! Move.

In terms of your business activity, you want to keep that moving too. Maybe right now you call two people a day. Go up a gear. Call five. Be in motion. Be constantly moving; because if you're moving you don't have time to doubt yourself. Just don't allow inactivity to slip in, because then you may start doubting yourself. Keep moving constantly to have that unwavering belief.

BLUEPRINT FOR SUCCESS

The Islamic blueprint is based on the seerah of the prophet SAW. That's his story. You can extend it to the stories of the companions he raised spiritually himself.

Now with the seerah, you will notice trends of success and that huge belief necessary for completing your goal. You see, most of those people, like Abd Al Rahman Ibn Auf left all their money to make hijrah. In Madinah they started again from zero. There they were coupled with Ansari sahaba. In Ibn Auf's case, he had Saad ibn Rabi', who had two wives and a lot of wealth. Saad offered Ibn Auf one of his wives and half of his wealth. Yet Abd Al Rahman Ibn Auf said keep both. Just show me where the market place is. He went and started trading. By the evening he had enough to buy himself food. In a few weeks, he was wealthy, all off his own independent effort.

These companions were very successful in their lifetime and used their wealth to secure a good place for themselves in Paradise.

There are four categories of wealth. The first is the person who has a lot of wealth and is using it in the path of Allah, in a righteous way. The second one is the one who does not have wealth, but is jealous of the person who is wealthy and giving in the way of Allah, saying "If I had the wealth, I would be giving too." The third is the person who is wealthy and is using it in an evil way, either sinning with it or harming others.

The final category is the worst of all. This is the person who is poor yet is wishing to be rich so they can do evil things, and is jealous of the wealthy person who is doing evil.

In that order, the first two are the best, and the last are the worst. Remember, the best of all of them are the ones that give in the way of Allah.

HE EARNED $2,000,000 IN ONE DAY

In the past, merchants were born into merchant families, most of the time. To this day, many entrepreneurs are entrepreneurs because they come from entrepreneurial families.

This goes to show that in order for you to become a merchant, or if you have little experience in learning new things, because being a merchant is different from being a consumer.

You see the day the iPhone 6 (a 2014 model of a smart-phone) launched, Com Mirza was showing how you could pull off a $2 million profit in a day. He capitalised on it by paying some managers to manage the buying and reselling. He made a deal with a friend in Dubai, and paid him to ship the phones to the Middle East. Seizing the moment and having an ambitious mindset were the keys. Instead of, "hey let me go buy the new iPhone," he thought:

"let me monetize the new release of this product."

- Com Mirza, CEO of Mirza Holdings

You have to dream and calculate. Take calculated risks. That's what the merchant does. Always asking how can I benefit from this? The mind is always thinking like a merchant. One of the easiest ways to start picking up their habits is just to hang out with other merchants.

Some people I met in Senegal, became merchants because they sat with other merchants long enough. It's the same process for other entrepreneurs that sell things. Be that in groups or companies. They are always selling; services, items, whatever it is, the process is the same. They are always trying to improve their margins of profits.

NO ONE STUTTERS HERE

Your vocabulary is learnt. Everything that you say nowadays; how you speak, the words you use, are learnt from your environment. School, parents, siblings.

There was a study done in Anthropology with a group of people in the Amazon. In that tribe, there was no word for 'stutter' in their vocabulary. And guess what? There isn't a single person that stutters in that tribe.

Do you see why it's important to eliminate certain words from your vocabulary? Especially words that are negative.

Your words create your reality. You have to eliminate the words of failure and doubt. Words like "this is not fair," "the world should be like this", "I am not sure" and so on don't serve you or your business.

Instead, use words of certainty like "I am certain", "there was a challenge and we will overcome it". Islam again gives an advantage to the entrepreneur. In a narration, the prophet SAW said that every morning the body parts say to the tongue to fear Allah for them.

Basically, if the tongue goes out of control, so will the other body parts. How is it for an exhortation to speak good about yourself first and your fellow people next?

Your vocabulary is learnt. Change your vocabulary and you will prosper. Malcolm X spent years and years memorizing the dictionary; every single word, because he knew that if you don't control what you say, if you don't know certain words, then you're easily manipulated. That is what happens to many people that watch mass media. Very often, words are manipulated to induce a different meaning. The word for what they want to say doesn't exist, so they cannot think the right way. It is very important to be articulate and know what to say.

One of the most articulate entrepreneurs I knew was Dr. Yaqub Mirza. He is a very intelligent man that is managing over $3.8 billion in assets. At one point, he was negotiating an important business deal with a less experienced person. During the negotiation, he was trying to buy a farm and some equipments. He used powerful arguments and started to overpower the other side. During the negotiation, he realized he was taking advantage of the other person because of his higher level of communication. So he stopped. That is the God consciousness of the true Muslim Entrepreneur; you have to know when to stop.

You can use your faculties and skills, like communication, and how to speak in an influential way.

Yet you also have to be God conscious and not exploit people in a win-lose situation. Always try to create a win-win scenario.

$300 MILLION MUSLIM CHAMPION

Your beliefs come from what you look at, people you talk to and the activities you do. So the first step is the things you look at. Are you looking at your goals? Mentally and visually? Is it clear to you?

I was just reading the story of the boxer Mike Tyson. As you know, he is a Muslim. He had a very turbulent life full of trials. Yet, what is remarkable about him is that he succeeded. He was taken out of drugs in crime infested Brooklyn to another school that was cleaner. He got into boxing there and went on to become the world's youngest heavy weight champion at 20. He went on to earn over $300 million. This all began with a change in his environment. That's how people win.

One other way to really change your belief is through the people you talk to. Are you talking to the right people? Maybe your ambition is to become an internet marketer. Well, talk to some marketers! Sit with a few millionaires and see what they do. Maybe your goal is to become a world class photographer. Then go talk to Peter Sanders. There is no other way. Talk to the right people.

Another way is to change your activity. Once you do this often enough, you will develop the right belief. I had some friends that would always tell me, "you do karate with so much ease, how is that possible?"

I always said, "I've been doing it for so long. Since I was 5. It's a hobby. That's why its so easy for me to do!"

When you do something week in, week out, it becomes a habit.

This goes for your business, as well. Keep doing it. You only need to follow these 3 steps to grow your belief:

Get into the right environment; talk to the right people; remove yourself from circumstances that don't serve you.

THE ART OF INFLUENCE

Influence is really just a transfer of belief. It's been said that the secret to success is to raise your belief. Set yourself up on fire, with enthusiasm. Then, when people show up, you build them up too because they see your enthusiasm. For most people, that kind of passion is attractive.

So how can you influence people? Talk to yourself in the mirror. Just talk to yourself and see if you believe in your dreams when you look at yourself.

What I've seen from my interviews is that so many of these entrepreneurs have faith in themselves. I remember asking Dr. Yaqub Mirza about what I should read whilst researching on Muslim business practices. He replied, "read my book!" And that's the kind of confidence a successful entrepreneur has. Develop that confidence. If you don't have it right now, that's fine. It takes time. But you can do it.

You have to have that self-promotional attitude. Promote your business. Promote what you do. That way you will succeed. I've seen it with Azim Rizvee. He promotes his business like nobody else can! That's what it takes to make it.

GOALS

THE POWER
OF THE
GROUP

1

THE POWER OF FAMILY

JINNADO

In Islam, the ties of kinship are known as silatul rahm. It is basically the family ties and they hold a great place in the religion. These ties are very strong. It's something sacred.

In every culture, people tend to respect these ties. Even the prophet SAW was accused by the Quraysh of breaking family ties. Yet, his response was "I came to strengthen the ties of kinship."

Linguistically, in Fulani culture, which is heavily Islamic, a parent is called Jinnado, meaning the one who was made to love. It's like they have had their hearts opened and love poured in. A parent cannot help but love their children.

That is why it doesn't matter if someone is a woman, a child or an elderly person; everybody you are related to through blood is very important and should be given their right.

Now, you as an entrepreneur can use those ties for tremendous wealth.

You see in business relations, people go in with self interest. Yet, there is something stronger than that. The ties of kinship have more power than even self interest.

The foundation of lasting wealth has to be built on strong foundations. Blood relations are the strongest foundations you can build on.

If you're after great wealth, pay attention. You have your idea, you've worked on your belief, you're starting to build your company. You have to learn how to use the ties of kinship and more generally the power of the group to further your enterprise.

WHO ARE YOU?

I'm not talking about race or nationality. Those define a very small part of your background. I'm asking the question: who are you? Who are the people you come from? What are their names? What were they like?

If you can't answer that, research it. Go as far as possible. This is your exercise for today. Research your genealogy.

I want you to invest in finding out as much as you can about your family. This is because your family is your first network. That includes your extended family.

You see, it's well known that certain traits are carried forward throughout generations. For example, my wife is an architect and likes to make things with her hands. The other day, I was asking her how she's so great at making things with wood, even though she hasn't been doing it for that long. She told me it's because her father, grand father and great grandfather all worked in their family business, which was carpentry. The skill has been in their family for generations.

Now what does that tell you? It tells you you're already naturally good at certain things. You can have a personal advantage if you are grounded within your family.

Say you come from a family of teachers, your core skill might be in teaching. As an entrepreneur, you can then get into entire industries that are based on teaching. There is network marketing, based on teaching people how to sell through mentoring.

There are people that are good with words. They grow up hearing people speak very eloquently and naturally inherit that. They might want to look into Law or Sales.

Look at Steve Jobs the late founder of Apple. He was a practitioner of esoteric religions. His dad was a Syrian Muslim and a self-made millionaire. Even though he was not raised by his biological father, Jobs inherited that drive and spirit, and most of all the belief that he could do it too.

So, look into who you are. Research what your family's strengths are. You may be different to them. But there is a big chance that you too are good at what others in your family are already good at.

So look into it and find out what those things are. Discover them. Emphasise them. Develop them. It will come to you naturally.

You may have heard of certain tribes that are predisposed to producing scholars. They memorize Quran more easily than others. People from those tribes have an environment around them where this task has been made easy for them, even if good memory isn't a genetic trait they've inherited.

If you grow up seeing everyone do something, you will develop the belief that you too can do it. If ten of your cousins are hafidh for example, it becomes very easy for you too because hey, everyone's doing it! Business is the same. If your family is in business, it becomes easy for you as well.
 So research your background and become grounded. Picture yourself as a tree. You want to dig your roots as deep into the soil as possible. That's when you can shoot into the sky. Like a bamboo tree that spreads its roots for a good few years without surfacing from the soil. The farmer may believe the bamboo plant is dead because he can't see any results. Yet suddenly, once it breaks the soil, within 90 days it shoots up to the sky and becomes 9 feet tall.

So picture yourself digging down into your family roots. Dig as deep as possible. You can gain strength from that.

TRIBAL POWER

I know it's not a very positive term nowadays, but what I mean by 'tribe' is the people around you. First and foremost, this will be your family. Your people.

Leverage your people and you will be using something greater than you. You are using the tribe to further your goals and help everybody around you in the process as well.

There is a big myth out there that you have to be a lone warrior as an entrepreneur. That myth goes like this: you have an idea, you go for it, even if you have to die for it! Believe in your idea even if no one is following you right now ... and so on. That may be true to some degree. Yet success doesn't just happen in that way.

Success, lasting success, is something deeply rooted within the ground. It has to have a firm foundation. So that you can shoot up to the sky from that foundation. A lone warrior doesn't have that foundation. A lone warrior will not succeed. Today, companies claim: "our CEO had an idea and suddenly became a billionaire"- yet, that is only one part of the story.

You see, people don't become successful overnight. Someone had an idea, I'm sure another person had the same idea, yet for one it worked out, and for the other it didn't. Most often, you just have to look at their financing to see where the difference lies.

Where did their money come from? Did it come from the tribe? Was there encouragement from the tribe? This tribe could be just their parents, or it could be other relatives, teachers and friends. Within their tribe, what are the relationships that furthered the goal of this so called lone warrior?

Once you dig deeper, you'll realize there is no such thing as the successful lone warrior. It is really the tribe that is working together. You have to know that once you start your business, your tribe, your people, will be the first to help. Even when the entrepreneur does not have apparent family support, they were probably supported to strive and get a great self-esteem at a young age.

You also have to realize that they are the first ones to believe in you because they know you so well. Careful though; they can also be the first to disbelieve for the same reason. But if you're going to be very, very successful, you want to make sure that those ties are strengthened. And that your people believe in you.

You may not be able to gain the financial support you need from them from the get-go, but at least come to some common understanding with them. If you're married, go to your spouse and talk to her (or to him). Discuss your goals, because they are out of the ordinary. If your goal is to become a millionaire or to create lasting wealth and not just get by with a job or small business, then the journey won't be easy. So you need that support. You will need that initial help.

Your investors may also look into your family support structure before they buy into your business.

If they find you have a strong backing, then they're likely to think "if the family is helping out, that means it's something I can believe in too." Because your family knows you better than anyone else. And once you get that help, you can start using exponential power. That way, it's not just you working anymore. It's you and so many other people. You're leveraging their brain power and ideas. You can also leverage their skills, their courage, their financial support. All kinds of things that will help you in your journey.

FAMILY LOAN

As entrepreneurs, we are very risk orientated. When the right opportunity comes along, we want to be first in line to put in our own money and our own savings, just to make the opportunity work.

Banks on the other hand, are risk averse. You'll experience this once you start your business. You'll find banks are not very willing to lend money to entrepreneurs. One of the reasons is because the entrepreneur may dream too big even if he does not have a solid track-record.

That is why your first resource is yourself. And then it's the people around you. This may be your spouse, your close family, brothers, sisters, extended family, and so on.

A lot of entrepreneurs I interviewed started out in this way. Shahzad Siddiqi started his law firm with a $10,000 loan from his brother in law.

He was able to get an interest-free loan in this way, and paid it off within a year. Even the richest man in Africa, Mr. Dangote, started with a 100,000 Nairas loan from his uncle, which is around 1,000,000 current US dollars. In this way he too started his business interest-free, and paid back his loan within a year. He was just 21 at the time and a fresh graduate of Al-Azhar University. He recalls fondly buying cartons of sweets just to make money while he was in elementary school.

As you can see, whether you are young or old, your tribe is your resource. So strengthen and utilize those relationships. Think of your family as your main safety net. When almost everyone else leaves, which will happen when the going gets tough, usually it's family that sticks around. They remain out of love to look after you; keep that in mind.

If you need money and your company is in financial difficulty, keep ties with your family open for help. We know most companies fail within one to five years because of a lack of funding. So try to solve that as soon as possible by strengthening the ties you already have.

IT RUNS IN THE FAMILY

As we mentioned earlier, you want to start your success journey by learning about those success patterns in your family. What are their strengths? What are their weaknesses? What skills are present in the family that you can leverage to further your enterprise? Cast a line on your family strengths to find out.

Mr. Hamdi Ulukaya did just that.

Though he came to America late in life. He learnt English only after migrating. An average Turk from a small kurdish village, his family had a yoghurt business. They had some livestock and used to sell milk from their cows. It was a simple family, a simple business. He continued working on a farm after travelling to the United States as a student. When his father came to visit him, he tasted the yoghurt his son was making at his new American farm. He was very disappointed by the taste. It was far inferior to what they had in Turkey! So he advised his son to open his own yoghurt business. Hamdi followed his father's advice. Within two years, he established a small yoghurt factory with basic equipment. It was mildly successful. Eventually, he bought a fully kitted out yoghurt factory, and grew exponentially. His brand today, Chobani Yoghurt, is worth multiple billions of dollars. It's so popular that I had no trouble finding some myself when I was in the States.

That tells you anyone can use family strengths. In his case, it was knowing how to work with milk and make amazing yoghurt. That was his family strength. As a yoghurt specialist, he didn't try to open a software company. He focused on what he knew.

You too can do the same. Find out what your strengths are, and even if your background is modest, you could have amazing success once you hone in on your strengths.

2

DO IT TOGETHER

LONE WOLVES DIE HUNGRY

I was discussing this with Imam Ashraf Zaghloul, whose company trades in the Toronto stock market. A tremendous entrepreneur, as we've seen. He told me this: "Oumar, if you're going to go into business, go in a group. Allah's hand is with the Jama'a. That is what most successful people do."

This advice may conflict with what we see on TV, which is the rogue entrepreneur going into business alone. That's a romantic idea; the initial idea may be from one person, but they have to find an alliance around themselves that propels them to success.

Allah is with the group (Jama'a). Success is with the Jama'a. So think about that.

The reason you'll want a group with you is that you can compress time frames. This is especially true if you go into business with someone that has strengths you don't have. Say, you want to sell software, but you only know how to write the code. If you go into business with someone who knows how to market and sell, this will help you. It will save you time. It will make your company very valuable because now you're leveraging other people's skills, other people's abilities, dispositions and strengths of character to further your goal. And you are all winning. That way, you can compress time frames.

Think about it this way: some software requires 10,000 lines of code. It would take you a very long time to do that! Say, you wrote 100 lines per hour, it would still take you 100 hours. Then if you had to correct any errors made along the way, it might easily take you 1,000 hours to complete a 10,000 line program.
Now, if you had two other people with you, this can be cut down to only 300 hours. So, you can literally get to your goal three times faster by having two other people help you. Do just that!

BILLION DOLLAR BROTHERS

Funding is the difference between success and failure. If you see an economy that's booming, the main component of the growth is funding. And it's the entrepreneurs that are getting funded.

In Islam, as we have seen before, when someone is invested into a business, they don't pay any Zakat on their investment. That's how Islam encourages going into business rather than just leaving money sit in the bank and accumulating interest.

So how do you secure funding if you're not from a wealthy family? Simple - go widen your circle by including your friends.

You can still pool these resources together. It would be easier if your family believed in you. I can tell you that it accelerates your success and reduces the possibility of failure. However, you need to be fair and give everyone a share in the business.

Imam Ashraf's younger brother, Dr. Hatim Zaghloul, headed a billion dollar plus company here in Canada. His fundraising technique was to pitch the idea to family, friends and his wider network. His inventions are responsible for the internet Wifi we use today.

He was pitching his invention to them and believed in himself very much while doing so. His belief was contagious. He had a huge vision, whilst staying realistic. He actually blew his goal out of the water!

He was expecting to have a $300 million company, yet ended up with a company worth over $1 billion.

His first pitch was:

"Invest $10,000 in my company, I will give you more shares than the people that will come in after you."

- Dr. Hatim Zaghloul, founder of Wi-LAN Inc.

And this was a huge incentive. To supplement these investments while the company was growing exponentially in the beginning, he got the cash he needed from other sources. He sold his house, he sold his car and several assets to gather revenue. He used all the funding he could get. This required tremendous support from his family. Especially his spouse and children. So have them on your side. Believe in your vision enough for them to believe.

Any enterprise will require capital to run and operate.

Your funding is your rocket fuel to success. How will you go to the moon without fuel? In the same way, if you don't have funding, your enterprise will die! Some are more capital driven incentives than others, but in general you should heed this principle.

NEED A HAND?

Then get mentorship. That's the first step. Get a mentor. Someone that can show you the way. This will save you time, money and energy.

How will you save time? Because that person has already been where you want to be. They have what you want to have.
So look for them carefully.

Whilst looking for the right mentor, consider the following: do they have the character you're looking for? Do they inspire you? Do they equip you? Do they know what they're doing? Do they have expertise and mastery in your chosen field?

I too have been blessed with mentors that have increased my self-belief tremendously. This gave me the courage to keep going in my business ventures and write this book. Ed Mercer, self-made billionaire and author of 'The 8th Grade Millionaire', told me one day, "young man, you're going to become a millionaire." That gave me massive self belief. We also discussed my beliefs on success at great length.

I've witnessed that if you get a mentor, you too can become successful, if you follow their advice. This is the main thing irrespective of how brilliant the mentor is, however rich. If you follow the advice, take massive action to move forward, and you're hungry to get the results you want, then you will succeed.

It's just a law. You're obeying the laws of success.

If you hear the information but you don't apply it, then it won't work out. So, it's critical to have a mentor that you listen to so you can save time and money.

An example of things going badly without mentorship is someone starting a chain of stores and locating somewhere where there is no crowd traffic. All that person will get is closed doors, even if they mortgaged their house for that store. It's purely a result of the lack of mentorship and advice. So ask for advice and people will tell you. Be open to ask.

If you ask, you will receive.

The successful Muslim Entrepreneurs are always asking.
For advice, for mentors, for help from Allah. Just call someone that you know can teach you what you want to know. Some are within your families already. These can be your strongest mentors because they know you so well. So if you have that resource close to you, go ahead. Because they are so close to you, they are also easier for you to look up to and relate to. Their success seems closer for you to attain the same too.

One Muslim Entrepreneur I interviewed who had an amazing family mentor was Salim Siddiqi. He told me how proud he was of his father, who was also his mentor and role model. His father left India during the partition with Pakistan and started his business from scratch. He eventually rose to become a leading engineer in the country.

He recounts how his earliest memories of his father was seeing him pray at night and asking Allah for help. That is profound.

Today, that same engineer's son is very successful and worth over $5 million dollars.

The lesson here is: optimism is transmitted from person to person. What would have happened if Salim's father had given up? The family would have learnt how to fail.

And let me tell you something that I heard from my mentor:

"Success is a habit and so is failure."

And that is one of the reasons why we are discouraged to broadcast our sins in Islam.

People come to know about those sins (failures) and may tend to repeat them, too. Yet, if it doesn't exist in their knowledge, they are less likely to do it.

In the same way, if in your enterprise, all you know is success, success will be natural. And that's what you want, for success to be the natural state of being. And being wealthy will not be a big deal; it will just be about contributing and about giving back. That is the natural state you want to be in to reach a very high level of success.

THE DREAM OF ISLAM

The biggest cause of failure is disunity. Disunity of hearts and minds. So have unity. Stay together as a Jama'a. The command for unity in the following ayat is repeated twice. Allah says:

"Hold firmly to the rope of Allah together and do not become divided."

- Surah Al-Imran, Ayah 103

This shows the strength we have in being united.

The second cause of failure is the appearance of success. The appearance of success might be a good position at work. Or fame. Or popularity.

I can tell you this: popularity, having a good image … it doesn't pay the bills. It doesn't pay for a car. It doesn't pay for a house. It's just fleeting popularity.

Money pays for those things. So look for that. If you want real success, don't follow the appearance of success. Follow real success, which are the principles here in this book.

Avoid success myths like "if you want to be rich, then you have to have a good job in that company, in that country." So many people have wasted lifetimes pursuing those myths.

Mr. Luqman Ali sees passed such myths. He is the founder of Khayyal Theatre. He is a very high quality director and creative visionary. One of the things we discussed in his interview was the American Dream.

You see, there is something called soft power.
Some countries use it better than others. America is the most well known for its use of soft power; through movies, popular culture, music and so on. America's soft power lies in its stories. The rags to riches stories. That is the concept behind the American Dream.

According to Luqman Ali, it's very rare to see a Muslim country with a discourse of dreaming at its centre.

That is why the two words "American Dream" are very powerful. Over time, it has developed an even greater attraction.

He does an exercise with young Muslims where he asks them "who knows the dream of Islam?" And most of them have no idea where he's coming from with that question! They'll come up with various ideas, but there is no unified concept. Yet if you ask the same kids what the American Dream is, they will come up with the same ideas and cultural references. He asks how is it that Islam is so important to you, yet, within you this dream doesn't exist? You don't understand the significance of this dream. And he goes on to teach the dream of Islam.

We want to ignite this dream again. What is the dream of Islam to you? Take 5 minutes to reflect on that, it will help you on your journey as a Muslim Entrepreneur.

SHARE THE SHARES

Now that you've created your company, you want to stick to the group. You do that by creating a common vision. That way, you all go in the same direction and avoid the group becoming divisive.

Once you have a common vision, your aim is to move together, in whatever you do. Stick to the group, even if there is no mutual agreement between all of you over a particular decision. Keep going. Go with the group decision.

Remember, you are only one person, while the group is more powerful. Even if the initial decision seems wrong to you, it might end up being right and correct itself along the way. If you go alone however, you are alone and there is no one else there to give you their perspective. You could end up swallowed up by the competition.

For Mr. Shahid Tata of the Tata Group, keeping the family business united meant going against conventional thinking. His textile mills were running with outdated Russian machinery and people thought the company would not survive. He aligned all the management to his vision for the company. Within a decade, the company was profitable and completely modernised. That is the power a solid vision can have. It defies all the odds.

Now, the third thing to know is that everyone has a good idea. That is one of Imam Ashraf's lessons. Everyone can come up with an idea.

You must have met people that are always sharing good ideas, yet never seem to achieve them. It must be very frustrating to be that person! How can you escape that? By going with your group! Don't be too protective of your idea. Instead, find partners.

One example Imam Ashraf gave me of the 'ideas-only entrepreneur' was when one person came to him for a business venture. He asked Imam Ashraf to invest in the business. Now Imam Ashraf is someone who has stock market experience, his company, NTG Clarity Inc. is publicly traded and he is massively successful. He's being asked by someone with zero experience, no rollodex of clients or following, to give his time, investment and energy.

In return, he was only offering Imam Ashraf 5% of his company. That's not very attractive for the Imam! Yet, the guy insisted that the idea was fantastic, that it was worth it.

The Imam's response was, "everyone has a good idea."

The lesson here is not to be unrealistic with your expectations of your investors. Work towards the dream realistically. How do you do that? Go into business with people that have experience and offer them real incentive to give you the advice you need.

Remember, it's better to own 1% of a $100 million company than to own 100% of a company in debt. So be open to sharing.

MUSLIMS MEAN BUSINESS

Teach success! If you have a Muslim brother, advise them in good. Advise them to start their own business. According to Mr. Mujeeb Ur Rahman:

"Every Muslim should start a business!"

- Mujeeb ur Rahman, Co-Founder Redco, Doha

That's encouragement right there.

Another way of encouraging good in others is to hide their faults. This was advice I was given from Ustadh Nouman Ali Khan. He assumes the best of these people. He genuinely thinks that the Muslims he deals with are the best and expects the best from them. And he gets those results!

For example, every year a small number of people tell him they can't afford the tuition fee for the course he runs, the Bayyinah Dream Program. He tells them they can still join in the class and pay the fees when they can afford it. Amazingly, 99% of these students will end up paying back the fee they couldn't afford at the start of the course.

This is because Ustadh Nouman believes people are intrinsically good. He expects only good, and receives that good. It's the process of getting what you expect.

He avoids suspicion. Even in his business, which is his main revenue generating activity.

He says:

"Give me what you can afford."

- Nouman Ali Khan, CEO Bayyinah

... and people end up paying in full.

This can work for your enterprise as well. As you secure clients, trust them and value them; see them as more than just numbers.
Value them like Ustadh Nouman. Then the doorways of success will be wide open for you.

Obviously, he is also savvy in his business dealings. The Muslim Entrepreneur does not allow himself to fall twice for the same mistake. If something is not working out, or someone is bringing negativity into his organization, he is also quick to put an end to that negative relationship.

3

GENERATIONAL WEALTH

YOU CAN'T INHERIT A JOB

Now you've started your enterprise, why would you want it to be generational? Why would you want to pass the wealth on to your children and your children's children?

You see, typically we are taught money is just one layer, which is us. You work for it, you make money now, then you spend it. You put in the hours, make money, spend it. Yet nobody can inherit that activity and its results.

Lets say you have a job, the most common way to earn a living these days. But nobody can inherit your job. I've never heard an employee say, "my dad had this job, now I am replacing him!" It doesn't work that way.

The child has to start over every time from scratch. You waste time that way.

The best way to build lasting wealth is generational. Zahoor Qureshi realized this, and it was one of his main incentives for leaving a well paid job in the City of London for his own Hobby Craft business.

Apart from passing on the business itself, the second step to make wealth generational is to teach success skills generationally. I've seen grandfathers teach their grandchildren success principles. Dr. Yaqub Mirza learnt how to run his business in this way. How to negotiate and close a deal. These are practical skills that can be learnt and taught to family first and foremost as a Muslim entrepreneur. Shahid Tata learnt the same way. So did many of the entrepreneurs I interviewed.

So leave your legacy. Give this book to your children. Read it as a family. Circulate it. Then you're not just teaching success to yourself. Otherwise, money can come very quickly. It can also go even quicker. Pass the knowledge down, deep into the family tradition.

Remember, there is a difference between the rich and the wealthy. "Rich" can mean a millionaire. Yet it's temporary. It's for a point in time. But what about wealth? Wealth is generational.
Wealth is when you don't have to work to maintain your income. When money is not an issue anymore. You can then focus on bigger things.

That's for people that have big, huge ambitions for themselves and their families. So learn how to become wealthy. Being wealthy is a mindset.

Families of wealth are talked about all the time. Great-grandfathers that were traders. Those traders passed on their money and skills, and kept them in the family. That's how true wealth has always been created.

GOLD, SILVER, DIAMOND

This is one of my favourite subjects- it's absolutely crucial! For the Muslim Entrepreneur, Islam has given you a framework of immense success. For example, the prophet SAW taught his companions to give good names to their children. It's crucial to give names with good, positive and uplifting meanings. This is one of the rights of the child.

How does this apply to success? Your name is something you will tend to hear more than anything else in your lifetime. Repetition reinforces things in the subconscious mind. So if your name has a good meaning, then you will naturally reinforce it and eventually embrace that meaning, embodying it.

That is one of the reasons why the name of the Messenger SAW: Muhammad or Ahmad, i.e. "the praise-worthy", is so popular. Not only does it have a good meaning, but it was also the name of an excellent role model. People embrace it whole-heartedly in hopes that their children too become righteous.

Now let's explore this principle to the next level. In my time studying personal development, I've studied in North America and Europe. I've met a lot of incredibly successful people. Not just Muslims, but Christians, Jews, Hindus etc.

That's when I noticed that a lot of wealthy Western Jewish families had changed their names. They didn't have Hebrew surnames like I thought they would. Their names were Anglicised. Names like 'Goldman Sachs'. When I was first developing my skills in Sales, I partnered with someone called Michael Silver. He was of Jewish origin.

You have Bob Diamond, CEO of Barclays bank. Gold. Silver. Diamond. These are all wealth-conscious names. Take a look for yourself - you'll be amazed at how an entire nation has been programmed for financial success. All the way down to the names!

What does this story tell you? It tells you that you and I have to realize Allah is Al-Razzaq (The Provider). He is the only One who gives and takes away.

How about Muslims? Do we apply the same principle? Yes, definitely. Malaysians for example call their country 'Rich Malaysia'. And look at the results! Malaysia is growing very fast, doing very well, full of Muslim Entrepreneurs that are very successful. So the Malaysians are following the Sunnah by giving a good, prosperous name to their nation. You too need to keep a good image of your people, your family and your children.

If not names, you can always give success oriented nicknames. It's a Sunnah that will lead you to prosperity.

GOLD-DIGGERS

Marriage in Islam is obligatory for anyone that has a desire for it. It's very liked by Allah and is heavy on the scale of rewards.

If I compare my results before getting married and after, I can see that I've grown a lot. You get more focused, especially if you choose the right spouse. And once you make the right choice, you have to be grateful for marrying the right person!

Why are married entrepreneurs more focused? Well, once you get married, you'll want to have children. This gives you a "why", something to work towards and some tangible goal to attain. Once you have children, you're now thinking long term, beyond yourself. What will they do when they grow up? You're considering the generations to come.

That is why Ibrahim (AS) made du'a for a progeny that will teach people good and purify them from evil. He also asked for sustenance for those future generations. He also asked for them to have an abundance of wealth. To this day, Makkah never goes hungry. They have a constant flow of income from the Hajj, even during the days before Islam was re-established in the city by the Prophet SAW.

Thus, marriage really is the start of all success. Around 95% of the successful entrepreneurs I interviewed were married and had families. It's something that really multiplies your wealth, in the literal sense.

You may think that if you have children you're dividing your income by all these dependents. But Allah gives you their Rizq too, and you find abundance instead of depleted resources.

Another motivation for having family as an entrepreneur is to have your own small Jama'a, that group you lead successfully. It's good practice for leadership. Without it, it may be difficult to lead a company with 100,000, or one million employees. It really starts with a small group you can lead successfully within the privacy of your own home.

So those of you that haven't gotten married yet- get married!

There are many examples in the seerah of how marriage brought wealth to the sahaba. One such companion was Julaybeeb. His family was unknown, he had no family or tribe to back him up. On top of that, he had physical deformities. He wasn't very easy to look at.

Julaybeeb was someone very vulnerable. Young and small with a humped back, with no tribe or protection. Yet, he was one of the strongest Muslims. The prophet SAW spent a lot of time with him. He joked around and was very kind to him.

One day, he asked Julaybeeb if he wanted to get married. The young man said, "yes, but who will marry me?" So the prophet SAW went and found a lady of great beauty for his companion and asked for her on his behalf. The parents of the lady were very excited to see the prophet SAW at their door, thinking he was the one proposing to their daughter.

But when they learnt the proposal was for Julaybeeb, they were horrified! "Anyone except him!" they thought. Yet the lady was so God-fearing, that when she heard them protest, she told her parents that if the prophet SAW had chosen Julaybeeb for her, she trusted Julaybeeb was indeed the best person for her.

Even though Julaybeeb had no money or tribal protection, that lady believed the prophet SAW and married him. Once the young man got married, he became extremely wealthy: one of the wealthiest men in the city.

What does this story tell you? It tells you that you and I have to realize that Allah is Ar Razzaq (The Provider). He is the only One who gives and takes as He wishes.

The story also proves that marriage is a means of prosperity for you. A happy marriage with someone you are dedicated to is something you want to look forward to as a Muslim Entrepreneur.

Secular research has also shown that married couples have tremendously more wealth than unmarried ones. In some cases, three times the net worth. They also tend to live longer. This is something to think about.

FAMILY PARTNERSHIPS

First of all, to build your enterprise, you have to find a good business partner. Who is the best partner? It depends. Sometimes family partnerships don't work, especially if there is incompatibility in character. But usually when people grow up together, they tend to think similarly, and it can work very well.

I've seen successful family partnerships working out for the entrepreneurs I interviewed. When it comes to family partnerships one example that jumps to mind is Dr. Munir Ahmed who is the CEO of Standpharm, a large manufacturer of generic drugs. Although trained as a medical doctor, he decided to help the family business expand.

The story begins with the father who started the business from scratch. Some pharmaceutical companies were looking for distribution so he acted as a distributor. In the second phase, the father started providing raw material to those same companies, representing overseas manufacturers and companies.

In the early 90s, he saw an opportunity to actually buy another company whose manufacturing licence was deregistered. And the company was almost dead. With that acquisition, the company established a good reputation and went on to be successful. We can learn from the Standpharm story that it is often a good idea to build the business as a family.

Muslim Entrepreneurs like the Zaghloul and Mirza brothers are extremely successful. Many of the 40 + entrepreneurs interviewed here, at least 60% of them, attribute their success to family. Sometimes it is a business that has the form of a partnership. Sometimes, it is just one person advising the other. In the case of the Zaghloul brothers, they were giving advice to each other. One brother gave advice on stock market offerings and how to take the company public. Their joint efforts ended up being profitable for the whole family.

Now, to start these relationships and maintain them, you have to manage expectations. Don't over-promise. But if the business is running well, then start a partnership so that everyone helps one another and can share in the results.Remember: nothing is perfect, but you can still make the best effort you possibly can, with eshaan. So the third step for that perfect family partnership is strengthen your own children for future potential partnerships. That is when parenting comes in.

Ask yourself how was your upbringing? Were you raised in a spirit of harmony and co-operation with your siblings? That is instilled from a young age. Did you ever feel some were favoured over others?

Did you ever feel you weren't loved as much as others? If you did, you can avoid these insecurities perpetuating further by making sure you are fair to your own children. A reasonably good parent will balance their time between all their children, daughters and sons alike, as Islam encourages.

PRINCIPLE VII

———————

WORK ETHICS

1

WORK, WORSHIP & FAMILY

THE ENERGETIC PROPHET

Work has a very high status in Islam. Work is blessed, and is the doorway to your rizq. Work is rewarded. In Islam, worship is not limited to the obligatory acts. Although the rituals are a very important part of worship. Work is considered a part of worship; an integral part. It is virtuous to be in action and be working. It is also the prophetic way.

All of our prophets worked hard for their living. They were all shepherds at one point in their lives. The wisdom behind that might be that it taught patience, how to lead a crowd of people, because they were responsible for their herd of sheep. Later, they were promoted to look after a flock of people. The shepherds of the past were independent people that were used to work in difficult conditions. They could be walking through a very dry, barren region to look for areas to graze.

An example is the prophet Musa (AS) whilst he was in the city of Madian. There, he came across two women that were the daughters of a righteous elderly man. He could see the difficulty they were in when they stood at the well waiting to water their animals. Musa offered to help them. When the women returned home, one of them suggested the father should employ Musa. They were assured by his trustworthy nature and strength. Both qualities are an essential part of work.

You can see from this that Musa (AS) was very competent with his hands. He had the ability to make things happen. In terms of work ethics, he was willing to work between eight to ten years just to marry the daughter of the elderly man he was staying with. That is great work ethic! There is no way someone lazy can be a prophet! It's the hardest job there ever is.

Therefore, work has a high status, it is a form or worship, and it is the way of the prophets. After tending to their flocks, they were also specialized in different professions: some were carpenters, others blacksmiths etc. All these very highly regarded in Islam.

TELL IT TO ME STRAIGHT

Correct information is so important. It constitutes your navigational system. It's very dangerous to have incorrect information when running your business. One of the traits of unsuccessful entrepreneurs is that they listen to the crowd. The crowd is rarely the richest or most successful. The crowd is rarely right.

If you study the world of investing for example, a serious investor will never buy an investment just because it is popular. But an investor will study the fundamentals of a business before he buys. It is that simple.

Don't listen to someone just because they love you. They may mean well for you, but are they really competent in the field you require to give you that information? Khalid Usman is a prominent entrepreneur and investor in the Toronto area. He credits his success to the fact that he does his due diligence for every investment he makes.

You will notice that some people will give you advice for free. Even before you ask for their opinion. But incorrect advice is very, very expensive. It may cost you your business, house, car- everything. Your business could go down if you listened to the wrong kinds of people. One of the principles of Islam is to "ask those that know if you don't know". So why would you ask someone that never ran a business or was never successful? Just don't do it!

So far, we've discussed emotion, belief and attitude. Now you know you need to work, but you need to take on the right activity. In order to do that, you need to know what to do. This will only come from the right information.

So if you want to become a millionaire, billionaire or whatever your goal for wealth may be, listen to someone that has already achieved what you want. Study how they speak, talk and interact with other people. What are their values, what kind of activities do they do, where do their children go to school? Study wealthy people. Ask for advice.

Another way to find the right information is by reading documents as well as the experiences of other people. You don't have to live a thousand years to get the right experience. Just read the right books about what the right people did. This will save you time and make you wiser in the process.

ENTREPRENEUR VS. EMPLOYEE

The main difference is that the employees expect a guaranteed pay-cheque. There is no guaranteed pay-cheque for the entrepreneur. Instead he believes he will earn his living by doing the activities he needs to get done.

If you have been to school for any length of time, then you'll know the traditional schooling system teaches you how to become an employee. And you can earn a good living from doing that. But if you want to be wealthy, you want to become really successful, and I assume that's why you're reading this book, then don't go for the paycheque. Go for the higher goal. This is one of the characteristics of Islam, to aim for the best. Why not?
Remember, the prophet SAW told us Allah has blessed trade. It is in the Quran, how Allah encourages trade; trade is good, it is virtuous and highly praised as a profession as a Quran.

As an entrepreneur, there is no ceiling on your income. You are essentially a trader. If you sell houses, as long as there are people being born, they need to live somewhere. So, it's a constantly growing market. If you're selling soap, when people shower they need soap.

These are a never ending supply-and-demand dynamics. As long as there are people, there is opportunity. Wherever you are in the world, you don't need to be in a particular country. You just need people.

Provide a need for those people, and there will be no ceiling on your income. As long as there are people, you will make a profit. No one can tell you: "you can only make 20,000 dollars this month." You could make billions, if that is your aim.

A good example is sir Anwar Pervez in the UK. He used to be a bus driver in Bradford. He isn't one anymore. As the chairman of the Bestway Group, he is a billionaire,. As a bus driver, he could only make so much a month depending on how many hours he drove, let's say that was sixty, eighty or a hundred hours a week. No more than that. If he was paid £20 an hour, and was working a hundred hours a week, the maximum he could earn in a week would be £2,000 which would be £8,000 a month. So, even if you work crazy hours, as an employee you are limited by time.

As an entrepreneur however, there is no limit. That is why he is a billionaire. He hasn't worked fifty million hours at twenty dollars an hour. What he did was build an organisation, a company, and leverage that system. Everybody that was in partnership with him, his suppliers, his employees, his executives, all got richer in the process, and he made a fortune for himself and his family, too. He didn't even have an education past high-school. He was a migrant from Pakistan; a "simple person". Yet he became a billionaire. You can do that too, by working as an entrepreneur and not an employee. No matter how good the job is, you're still an employee, and you can't get wealthy that way, unless you use other systems like investment, which we will come back to.

2

ETIQUETTES OF THE MUSLIM ENTREPRENEUR

SOW NOW REAP LATER

Recall Imam Ashraf's 'Ayah of Success' :

Those who wish for the Hereafter, and strive with all due striving, and have Faith - they are the ones whose striving is acceptable to Allah.

-Al-Quran, Surah Al Isra, Ayah 19

In this ayah, Allah instructs us to believe, firstly in Allah, and then do the work. You conceive the idea, believe in it, then you do the activity.

When we discussed belief earlier, we said belief affects your results, the correct belief can make you rich. Belief gives you the right mindset. It will allow you to see opportunities where other people were not able to. Once you set your body and mind in motion, you will start working towards your goal. It may be that you start by talking to people, getting sales, building your product and so on…

Whatever it is, you have to have the 'Farmer Mentality.' The Quran talks a lot about the farmer, and how he plants a grain. Allah says;

> "And have you seen that [seed] which you sow? Is it that make it grow, or are We the Grower?"

-Al-Quran, Surah Al Waqiah, Ayah 63-64

There are a lot of ayahs about how a farmer grows his crop from the rain. Once they harvest what grows, some are thankful, and others forget that Allah was the source of all their positive results.

First and foremost, they plant. They plant, and then take the reward. This is a law Allah has created. You must use it to your advantage if you want to become successful. Plant first. Reap later.

DOING YOUR BEST IS NOT GOOD ENOUGH

Have you noticed some people in your local community are constantly in demand? People come and visit them, people ask them for help, people need them all the time.

Somehow, many of these kinds of people are very, very prosperous too. It doesn't matter what they do, really. It can be someone involved in the masjid like an imam, or an entrepreneur, or someone always helping people around them. Somehow, you notice that everything seems easy for that person.

Well, the real secret of people like that, and I highly recommend you study what they do, is that they give more. They give and give and give, and eventually it comes back to them. Multiplied.

One way to give more is to give whatever you're doing a hundred per cent of your attention whilst doing it. You may not be involved in a business full-time, you may still be working for someone else. According to Azim Rizvee, if you're working for someone else, give it a hundred per cent of your effort, don't be doing something else on the side, especially during work hours. He got his start as an employee and would show up at night to help out the team in case of emergency. Whilst you're working for someone else, or while you are volunteering for your local masjid, or helping relatives, focus on the task. Whatever it might be, give it a hundred per cent. This habit will really boost your business. Always give more of yourself.

You want to set a standard that's so high that others will be measured by it. By that, I mean, as an entrepreneur, you want to set a standard of work ethic that is so lofty that others want to emulate it. If your employees see their boss slacking off for example, then they will do what you do. Remember you are the leader.

There is an attitude in Islam known as Ehsaan; to do excellence.
The prophet SAW said Allah loves what is done properly, with ehsaan.

So even when you slaughter an animal for Eid or an Aqeeqah for example, do it well by making sure the knife is sharp enough so it doesn't hurt the animal. This principle applies to everything we do.

To do Ehsaan means to do good quality work. And quality is assurance. Why do you think people may prefer a BMW to a Kia or a Hyundai after all? Because they know the BMW car is well made. They know the company has invested a lot of effort in developing their product, and the price is worth it. Why is it that people will spend thousands of dollars on a wedding gown? Because they know it's really well made.

There is a lot of artistry that goes into it, a lot of sweat, hard work, design and skill. That shows in the price tag. When you do good work, it will show and people will buy. So whatever you do, do it excellently. That is something that will make you look forward to what you produce.

Don't just do your best. As an entrepreneur, doing your best is not enough. Your best, might not get you to where you want to go. If you think about it, sometimes, lets say in the investment world, someone like Dr. Yaqub Mirza is competing with an entire field of investors.

These investors are big firms, Fortune 500 companies and mutual funds that are investing people's money. But now he has taken leadership in North America when it comes to Halal investing, and beyond that, the kind of investing that is morally and ethically conscious.

He has made it a rule to only invest in companies that are beneficial to society and produce goods that will enhance people's lives. For him to become successful, he had to take care of competition.

So he gave a very high quality, reliable product, and one of the key things I noticed was he was results-oriented. When I look at the performance of his investment of his mutual funds, they were averaging over 13% a year, which is very high considering that there was a financial crisis in that time. Despite that he continued to grow and people were making money.

So, whatever your line of business is, if you're not seeing results, say to yourself: 'I don't want to do just my best.' Because your best might not be enough. What you want to do is what is necessary. The necessary to achieve the result. Let's say you want to sell a product - you'll see me discuss Sales a lot because I'm involved in it myself. Almost every entrepreneur has to sell a product at some point; that's what private companies do.

When I started in Sales, I was knocking on a hundred doors per day. The pitch was very fast. It was a small product. That was my first experience in direct sales. But that was not enough. What was enough, what was necessary was to knock on 200 + doors per day. Once I visualised this goal, I started to surpass all of the competition, everyone in the company.

My sales were off the chart, everyone was really surprised. You too can really increase your numbers and the results will come. Just work more than your competition to see the results, especially in the beginning.

THE POWER OF COMPLETION

The Power of Completion lies in completing every single project you take on. You can review daily with your team or even your spouse. Review what you're doing and reflect on the future. Now that you have a game plan in place, you have your goals, you have energy, you have a partnership going, you've launched your business, you may start getting a few results. To get even bigger results, you have to yield the power of completion.

What is completion? The power of completion is to close down what you started. If you started a degree, finish it! Even though education is not an obligation, many entrepreneurs don't finish high school for example, but when they start a project of their own, they finish it because they are passionate about it. Don't leave a project half way just because it's difficult. Stick around until it's concluded, even if it concludes in a failed attempt. Otherwise without a result you will have lost time, lost energy and lost self-esteem.

You want to finish what you start. Once you get a habit of completing what you started, you can achieve any goal. All you have to do is just finish smaller goals and projects to reach the bigger ones. Constantly keep an eye on the future, learn from past mistakes and adjust your course of action.

An exemplary application of this principle is Mr. Shahzad Asghar, CEO of Style Textiles. He completes what he starts, always. That is one of the character traits of really successful people. When he delivers, he tries to deliver with Ehsaan. He is producing the material used in sporting equipment by companies like Nike.

His strategy is to always deliver on time with over 98% accuracy. He keeps to quality standards and his promised shipping times. He is on top of his game in this way.

This concept of completion is being applied by Mr. Farouk Sheik. I was talking to him after a lecture on entrepreneurship. A very enthusiastic young Muslim from France joined our discussion. That person had several projects going. Farouk heard all his proposals. Afterwards, he told him: "if you want to be successful, stick to one thing. Stick with one course of action until you become successful." That shows how savvy Muslim Entrepreneurs behave. They have a single purpose and they focus. That is how they become successful. They complete all the projects they start. If it fails, they scrap it and move on to something else..

15 HOUR WORK DAY

To have great work ethic, keep your desires high. A sign of low desire is to be sleeping all day, or have wishful thinking. This can happen to all of us. Someone with a low drive is always dreaming about things but is really not doing what is necessary to make his vision a reality.

That shows the desire is not there. The goal stays a wish.

Think about a child that wants a bicycle as a present. Their parents say, "no you're not ready for this."
The child insists, and it's all he can think about all day. Every time he goes outside, he notices other children on a bicycle.
It makes him think, "wow! I can't wait to get a bicycle, how can I get a bicycle?" That's true desire. It's not corrupt. He just wants that bicycle; it's his dream.

Eventually, the child repeats his request so persistently to his father, even though months go by, he keeps asking, "what do I need to do to get a bicycle?" The father sets the condition that the boy has to do well in his studies to get the bicycle. What do you think the child is likely to do? Study hard! He could be up at one in the morning just studying, even if he doesn't like it. Eventually he gets the result he needs: a new bicycle. His desire enables him to achieve his goal.

In order for you to have great work ethics, keep your desire high, and hang around energetic people so you don't lose your energy. Hang around people that are positive, that are entrepreneurs, always on the go making things happen.

In the beginning, you may have to work long hours. That's something I learnt from Mujeeb Ur Rahman in Doha, who runs REDCO, a huge construction company in the Middle East and Pakistan. His work ethic is incredible. He advises people to work for around fifteen hours a day.

Just like that child always thinking about his bicycle fifteen hours a day, you want to be thinking about how to be successful for long periods of time. You will achieve your goal that much faster.

CHARGE LIKE A RHINOCEROS

This is really one of my favourite comparisons; seeing a high energy entrepreneur as a rhinoceros. Allah has created all these animals, all these creatures as examples. In the Quran, Allah praises those-

"Who remember Allah while standing or sitting or [lying] on their sides and give thought to the creation of the heavens and the earth,"

- Al-Quran, Surah Aal-Imran, Ayah 191

That is one of the benefits of the creation of Allah.

Now a rhinoceros is always charging, always going despite the obstacles. A rhinoceros is enthusiastic, it is outgoing and energetic. That is what you want to do as an entrepreneur. If you want to get funding and your enthusiasm is lacking, your investors won't want to get involved. So develop the enthusiasm, the energy of a rhinoceros and see what it does for your success.

An example of a very energetic entrepreneur is Com Mirza. He is always bursting with energy. Sometimes, it comes across even on social media. If you're building a business, I really recommend using social media to create an online presence. Com is building his business and always writing long social media posts that keep track of what he is doing. Being a serial entrepreneur, his first success was with a car dealership software and he expanded into all kinds of areas.

He has so much energy, it is contagious and exciting. It's something that rubs off on you. This is something I've noticed with successful Muslim Entrepreneurs. They tend to do a lot!

Mrs. Oumou Ndiaye is the same. She is at the head of a successful company that makes software for customs. Although she is a mother, she has a lot of energy and I can tell you it is contagious. Keeping up with deadlines can be stressful for your team so you need to give them that boost of energy.

I do not recall a single serious business owner that is not energetic and passionate; none of them are dead-beat, sucking the energy around them. One of the virtues of having enthusiasm is being the kind of person that gives life. So that people are always feeling better in your presence; better about themselves, about their goals. That is the kind of person you want to be eventually. Develop that mindset.

3

BE EFFICIENT

SUCCESS IN THE PIPELINE

People say "I want to start my business, but I'm worried I won't know how to balance my life with my work. I don't want to be working all the time."

There is a given time for everything. Islam teaches us this discipline. For example, when the time of prayer comes, we are ordered to abandon trade.

In the seerah, the prophet SAW was once giving a khutbah on Jummah and some companions were still rushing to their trading caravans. This is not allowed.

When the adhan is called, everyone leaves everything and prays. Surat Jummah was revealed in that occasion. So there is a time for everything.

In the same way, family has a right over you as an entrepreneur and worker. It's not just about bringing in the money and the goods. People need time to develop around you. If no time is spent, affection can be lost.

So, in order to become extremely successful, you don't just have to put in the hours, which is what it takes, especially in the beginning. Your success will come from the structure of your business. The structure of your business can give you time freedom. It's not highly recommended to get into a small restaurant business structure, for example. You may be the greatest cook ever, but if you're operating alone, serving as well as cooking, you will be putting in a lot of hours. That's just not conducive to a balanced work-life routine.

If you did want to start a restaurant successfully whilst having time freedom, you would look into a franchise system instead. This allows you to pay royalties to people in order to use their existing, successful systems. That is what McDonald's did. In the Muslim Entrepreneur market, Mr. Tariq Farid has done the same. He is chairman of Edible Arrangements, a company that sells fruits dipped in chocolate arranged beautifully as flower-shaped bouquets.

I interviewed one of his franchisees. Tariq Farid's business really grew once he utilized the franchise system, and now they are doing over half a billion dollars in annual sales, which is a fantastic amount. So get your structure right, that way you will not have to do all the work yourself.

Let's say you want to carry water from an uphill water source to a nearby village. There are two ways to do this. One is to get lots of buckets and carry it by hand, bit by bit.

This is a tiring way to go about things; like in a small business. The smarter way would be to build a pipeline that will carry the water for you, so you don't have to work all those hours.

Obviously you will have to build the pipeline in the beginning, which is where all the hard work lies. After that, you can relax.

What will really give you the freedom of time, to focus on other important things in your life, is the structure of your business. Study the structure, and results will follow.

DON'T WASTE MY TIME!

Manage time wisely. One of the shortest surahs in the Quran says:

"By time. Indeed, mankind is in loss. Except for those who have believed and done righteous deeds and advised each other to truth and advised each other to patience."

-Al-Quran, Surah Al-Asr

Now you do not want to waste time on what is not important. It's not just about working, but working with the right aim and reason in mind.

That is why we talked so much about "Intention" at the beginning of this book.

If you have the right intention and do the work for the right reason, and the work will be worship for you.

People that waste time are involved with play and desire. They are involved in idle talk. This is criticised in the Quran. Keep in mind that even in Paradise, there will be no gossip or vain talk between the inhabitants. In Jannah, Allah SWT will only allow beneficial discussions to take place.

Avoid wasting time, on social media for example. There is nothing wrong with having a social life. But if you find yourself engulfed in those things, just look around and see how successful people manage their time around the social media phenomenon. How are they using social media to their advantage? If you want a different result, do what the successful Muslim Entrepreneurs are doing. Manage time effectively and see how successful you will become. Be possessive about your time.

Whilst doing all this good quality work, you may be thinking about work-life balance again. How will you find the time? Remember, it comes down to time management. You don't want to just be doing "busy" work.

Busy work might be, as a salesman, checking your attire, repeating your pitch a hundred times… that will all give you practice. But what will give you more practice? Repeating your pitch in front of a mirror or going out there and pitching to a real customer? A real customer! You might fail a few times to begin with, but at least you talked to a real customer.

That's what you want to do; just get out there, practice, practice, practice.

And then see what will happen.

As the saying goes:

"Practice does not make perfect. But practice makes better."

One of the key tips I learnt from listening to successful Muslim Entrepreneurs is that they keep time for their Akhira as well. Some pray at night. It is not easy to form this habit. But all I know is, it is important when you want to ask Allah to make things happen in your business, in this life and in the afterlife. Pray at night and ask. The Muslim Entrepreneur is the one praying at night and asking Allah for help.

I was told this by Arif Mirza whom we mentioned before. This is a big secret tip from him. He sometimes asks so much that people inquire: "why do you ask for so much, Arif?" His reply is: "Allah is so great, what is a few million dollars to Him? What is what I'm asking to Him?" This is the mindset of abundance. Allah can do anything, so why not ask?

Manage your time wisely, during the day and at night and see how your business will grow, your spirituality will grow- everything you do will experience growth.

LIFT-OFF!

They say money is attracted to speed. If you want to start your business, a critical component of it is speed.

You want to reach profitability before you go down, so to speak.

If you reach profitability early on, you will stand a higher chance of surviving in the long run.

When you start your business, don't just think "I'm going to try this and see how it goes."

You have to have a higher level of commitment than that, and put in a lot of energy right at the very beginning.

In network marketing, the first week is really the most important week, even if the business is to last ten, thirty or four hundred years. This is because the first week builds belief, creates momentum and a lot of energy around it.

The same stands for when you start a restaurant. The first week, you want to invite all your friends and all the people in the neighbourhood. Many people should be present at the launch.

You have to also be prepared and increase the belief, the excitement; and there are ways to do that. Once you acquire the customers, there are a whole lot of marketing techniques that you can implement to retain them. Study those techniques in order to launch properly.

Put most of your energy, 80% of it, in your launch. One of my mentors told me it's like going to the moon. If you want to take off, you want to put 80% of the energy right at the beginning so you have enough speed to exit the stratosphere, so to speak.

You see it everywhere in the investment world. When a company is launched into the stock market during the initial offering, there is a lot of excitement going on. Many articles are written, there is a lot of press; all to ensure the company gets the most funding, the most attention.

You want to do the same at a micro level. Launch properly. Don't just announce what you do. Promote it.

MONEY LIKES SPEED

Another key to a good work ethic is urgency. Realize that you don't have a hundred years to become rich. If you did, then you could have just been an employee, saved the money, invested it … you could make something happen by halves here or there. But an entrepreneur spots opportunity and acts on it immediately.

We talked about how to launch properly. You want to go fast, build it quickly. In most businesses this is the case. You lost money? Make it back quickly. You have to think about all the people you have to help once you become very wealthy. They need the money quick, don't they?

One of the character traits of successful entrepreneurs that I met is that they decide very quickly. They don't tend to go back on their decisions. They trust their gut instincts. They go for it. And you want to develop this trait, too. Have urgency. Make decisions fast and move forward. Don't be someone that is always planning and stuck on perfecting their business plan.

Sure, have a business plan and a roadmap for your enterprise, but always move fast into action. This is almost as important as the plan; get the execution going and get results, so that you have numbers to show for your effort.

When we talk about investing, you'll see that a lot of investors want numbers. So if you are working on a venture and you don't have any numbers, it's hard for an investor to do anything if he is serious.

That's because you only have speculation and no grounds for proving anything. Get some kind of result, even if it's small to begin with, so that you know how the market is, and then proceed. And always move fast.

I often hear people say, "I want to become somebody, I always knew I would become somebody, I just want to become someone important." If that's the case, then just act on it! If you want to become an entrepreneur, just do it! If you want to quit your job and work for yourself, just do it! If you want to become successful, just do it! Act on your intention. The results are from Allah. Therefore, move fast, with energy and conviction. Just do the actions required and you'll see the results.

THE 15-MINUTE DIAGNOSIS

You have to learn how to work effectively. Dr. Amina Coxon is a British doctor that trained in John Hopkins; one of the best hospitals in America. She was a born Christian, but was always very inquisitive. She became dissatisfied with that faith. At age 50, she saw in a dream a light leading her to the Kabah. That is when she found Islam, 23 years ago. I'm telling you this story so that you gain an appreciation for the kind of person she is.

Once a patient visited her with a complex condition that would require any average doctor at least an hour to diagnose and treat.

She did it all in 15 minutes.

Her X-Ray technician was bemused at the speed of her diagnosis, and called her up to ask if she needed to see the patient again. He was completely shocked and amazed by the efficiency of Dr. Coxon. She has gained this efficiency by completely mastering her subject. She is using her mastery to make decisions quickly and efficiently.

She told me her secret :

"I've learnt my subject thoroughly, even though I hadn't seen the condition he had in 20 years, I learnt it thoroughly. So learning how to learn is so important."

-Dr. Amina Coxon, Harley St. Physician

Remember that, especially for those of you who want to be entrepreneurs in the knowledge industry. Learn how to learn. Then focus. She recommends reading the book 'Learning How To Learn'. One of the main tips Dr. Coxon learnt from that book is that the brain cannot learn for more than one hour at a time. The best way to learn is to do it in focused learning chunks.

HUNT WITH THE PACK

Now that you know you must balance between life, work and ibadah, the real question is how to delegate. You don't want to be running a single person restaurant, cooking all the time.

You don't want to be washing all the cars in a car-wash by yourself. You want a system where a lot of people are doing simple tasks and everyone is making money to let you take off and become free.

When it comes to your business, that's called delegating. That is one of the characteristics of a leader. The prophet SAW said the hand of Allah is with the Jama'ah. That's something I heard from Imam Ashraf.

When you go into a venture, it's usually a bad idea to go in by yourself. I know we're sold the tales of lone entrepreneurs that became millionaires by themselves. But really, just study great companies that people admire. Study the entrepreneurs around you. Very often, you will find they will go into ventures in groups. They will have investors behind them, backing the project. People with different skills, people with different points of view. Do exactly that. Delegate. Believe in others.

You can't just say this is a single man project and do everything yourself. That is the model of a very small business; the recipe for being limited! If you want your business to grow, you want to have a whole lot of people that are helping you achieve that goal while you help them achieve theirs.

To develop your skill on working in a group, I highly recommend you to look into network marketing. It will allow you to learn people skills. Learn how to work in a group towards the same goal.

Once you have your group delegated, you have to become irreplaceable. Let's say you have two, three, five partners going into a venture. If you don't want to be replaced anytime soon, and you don't want the venture to go down, then make sure every single one of you is irreplaceable so that the partnership makes sense.

Very often people will associate simply with people they like. That is only one criterion of picking a partner.

Typically if you like someone, you will have the same strengths and weaknesses. You want to associate with people that are different from you so they can compensate for your weaknesses and you can do the same for them.

For example, if you're a scientist, partner with a lawyer. They can take care of the writing, while you do the math. Find a partner to complement you and delegate the tasks accordingly. You will grow.

HOW TEENAGERS RUN A BILLION DOLLAR ENTERPRISE

Many times, a system will either make your business strive or stagnate. We don't want stagnation. The title of this book is Success Principles of the Greatest Muslim Entrepreneurs, after all. We discussed how to prioritise between family, work and akhira.

As an entrepreneur, systems are key to this. Systems will free your time. S.o design a good system.

One of the things I learnt from Imam Ashraf is that the small fish always wants to protect his or her idea. So they protect their idea and work on it alone, and remain small because of that. The small fish is thinking, "if I talk about this idea, someone else will pick it up and do it first, then I won't be successful."

So they protect their idea and work on it alone, and remain small because of that. We don't want that. We want an attitude of abundance. Share it everywhere. If the person is a true entrepreneur, they are probably too busy to take on your idea, they're too busy doing their own thing and have their hands full already! If they aren't a successful entrepreneur, the chances of them taking your idea and making it successful are very slim, because if they are not already successful it is probably due to a lack of work ethic, experience or ability. So you have nothing to lose. Go out there, share your idea, get investors, get partners, make it work. Work with a Jama'ah, the hand of Allah will be with you.

Partnerships are a way to create a good system. So get help. Get help from people that know how to run a business, raise money in the stock market-whatever you need. It's teamwork that will allow you to level-up.

I like to give the example of kebab shops. A kebab shop is a small business, just one person serving very good quality kebab. Now taking this to the next level would be a McDonald's-like model. It's a business that is systematised. Teenagers that you would not trust to run the house over the week-end can run a multi-million dollar McDonald's franchise.

So get a system going. A system will allow you to save time, energy and effort. One of the characteristics of rich people is they like to do boring things. A rich person may be doing the same thing for twenty years, whilst a not-so-rich person jumps around all over the place. Today, the average career in North America lasts less than four to five years.

Therefore, you be the exception. Be the Muslim entrepreneur that does not know the meaning of the word 'recession' and has a big impact on society.

PERSISTENCE

&

HABITS

1

KEEP GOING

GET BACK UP AGAIN

One of the most important attributes in Islam is persistence; the attitude to keep on going no matter what happens.

You see, when people are tested with some difficulty, that's when you will know those that have real endurance from those that were just pretending. When times get tough, a lot of people give up on their dream, seek employment, find another way, change lines of business- anything, instead of persisting.

Persistence is what was pushing Mujeeb Ur Rahman in Doha. Despite going through prison, being faced with life threatening situations, despite people stealing millions from his business and damaging his reputation, he persisted.

Such hurdles can come up against anyone on their path to success. That is because the more successful you are, the more resistance you may find. The more competition you may find. So if you find that no one is criticizing you, it may be because you're not doing anything significant.

Mr. Rahman had that glamour life. He was making huge amounts of money. Then all of a sudden, at the age of forty, he found himself in jail, where he realized: "wow, I've been working since my twenties, yet here I am, despite being very successful." He told me at one point, even the Finance Minister of his country would line up outside his office just to see him. Yet once in prison, he tried to contact those former friends, but nobody would attend his calls.

No business contact was valuable for him in his time of need. Imagine such a dire situation. That was when he really took his attitude to the next level. There he was, with all those contacts, yet they could not benefit him. It was time to make a change. From that time, he committed to spend more time with his family and also learn the Islamic religion.

Even though he would be building up his business from scratch again, he believed the ultimate control was with Allah. He prayed for big goals and big dreams. And you know what? Despite the difficulties he faced, he still believes that every Muslim should go into business. That's a tremendous statement to make! Why? His attitude is: 'no matter how many no's I get, I'm going to keep going.' Take the no's and the rejections. Get up, and do it again anyway. That is persistence.

Mr. Yaya Ndianor, a Senegalese entrepreneur that owns a large umbrella of businesses had a similar experience.

With his brothers, he embarked on a trip to the Congo to make a fortune. Their business grew quickly. However, war broke in the region and they had to flee the country at gun point. Thanks to their perseverance, they recouped their losses quickly.

THE MYTH OF SUCCESS

Some people tend to assume Muslims that become extremely successful got there through a special Dua, or Qadr, or because they were born smart. They might think, 'they just got lucky', or 'they have connections'.

If you thought any of that, then the examples I have provided in this book should prove to you that their success came from none of these things.

The most successful Muslim Entrepreneur is no different from you and me. If you operate with integrity, and follow the ethical rulings of trade in Islam, then there really is no difference between you and a successful Muslim Entrepreneur.

An entrepreneur is a person working with capital.

Some of them are born into wealth, like Aliko Dangote, whose grandfather was already the wealthiest man in Nigeria. Mr. Dangote took it a step further and is now the wealthiest man in all of Africa.

But there are also people like Dr. Mirza, who wasn't born into tremendous wealth. He just migrated to America, and now a few years later he is at the head of a $3 billion company, producing a very high return and doing great things.

We also met Dr. Miles Davis, who had most of his friends either shot or in prison. His story was very emotional as he explained how Islam saved him from all of the drugs and corruption of the streets of America. Today, he sits at the board of major corporations and is the dean of a business school focused on entrepreneurship.

Then, you have people like Sir Anwar Pervez, who used to drive buses in England. He immigrated, didn't have much of an education, hardly went to school, and yet is now at the head of a multi-billion dollar enterprise, the Bestway corporation, which he started from a single grocery shop.

So as you can see from these examples, there are people that started off rich and became very rich, but also people that started off poor and with very little education, yet they too get those massive results. So if you thought it was about their level of education; no. It's not that. There are PhD graduates working for Sir Anwar Pervez, who didn't even finish high-school.

Remember that one of the names of Allah is Al-Razzaq, the Provider, and He gives to whoever He wants. So you have to realize that nobody is special. All that we have was given to us, as an opportunity to do good. It is vital to give back to the community, to give back to the people around you, to give back to the Muslims and to whatever country you're in right now.

That is why there are Muslim Entrepreneurs building hospitals, schools and mosques in America, the Middle East, Africa- all over the world! So the real deal is this: Allah is eternally Rich and He gives to whoever He wills without decreasing even a little bit in His wealth.

That is why a successful Muslim Entrepreneur is just like you and me. All they were given is from Allah. To think you have to have some special gene is a myth. They are favoured with certain blessings, yes. But you too have a hidden talent. These entrepreneurs go to sleep, have families etc; they don't have extraordinary capabilities or knowledge. So believe in Allah and believe that He will give you what you need to become successful and help you fulfil whatever goal you have.

DEFEAT IS TEMPORARY

This life is temporary, so really, no defeat is permanent. Everything is temporary. So some people may think they are winning but they may be losing in terms of the next life. This is a powerful reality check.

You have to have the right intention; help your family; help people, change lives, change your community. These are all very noble goals. To help your family first and foremost is the noblest of them all. Maybe you'd like to buy them a big house. Whatever the goal is, as long as it's allowed in terms of Shariah, move forward with it. If you fail, think of it as only a temporary failure, but if you persist, success will come.

I'll remind you again of Imam Ashraf's favourite ayah on success; if you persist, and you believe, then you will see success. It comes back to what your core value system is.

If you find yourself faltering after a setback, go back to the chapter on 'Belief'. Re-grow your belief. Your belief in Allah first of all, then yourself, your company and your product.

Sheikh Hamza Yusuf reminded me of the ayah:

"The believers have already succeeded."

-Al-Quran, Surah Al-Mu'minun, Ayah 1

If you are already successful, then failure cannot be an option.

An example of the seera illustrates this point. When some of the prophet SAW's companions made the migration (Hijrah), they were tremendously wealthy, like Abdelrahman Ibn Auf and Usman Ibn Affan. But when they migrated, they lost all their money. They were kicked out from their birth place, Makkah, and they went to Madinah to protect their faith. Now how often do you see people migrate and lose all their wealth for their religion? Nowadays, people migrate for different reasons: to pursue wealth or because of the fear of poverty.

When the Muslims arrived in Madinah, the migrants were coupled with the Ansar and the prophet SAW made them brothers in faith. They gave them homes and jobs. They were brothers despite not sharing lineage or family, yet they could inherit each other's property whilst the Muhajiroon were new to Madinah.

So Abdelrahman Ibn Auf's brother, Saad Ibn Rabee', told him, "I have all this wealth, and you are my brother. I know you came by yourself, left your family behind, with no money and no wife, so what I'm going to do is give you half of my wealth and choose who to marry from my two wives after I divorce her for you." That is how generous they were; the Ansari were willing even to give up their marriage and half of their wealth for the sake of their religion.

But what did Abdelrahman Ibn Auf say? He said:

"May Allah bless you in your wives and success in your wealth. Just show me where the market place is."

And then he went to the market place and started business. He would get a customer, get a deal going and make a commission. He did that for just one day, and he already had enough to buy his own food. The next day he did the same, and he started buying things, like a donkey. Within a month or two, he was already pretty rich.

One day, the prophet SAW saw him sitting on a roadside after a long time, well dressed and fragrant with the scent of a woman. The prophet SAW asked him why that was so. Abdelrahman Ibn Auf told him he had just gotten married. The prophet SAW inquired about the dowry he had given. He told him he gave a sa' (a large quantity) of gold. So he was rich; within a few months. What does that show us? That he had the attitude of a successful Muslim Entrepreneur. Despite his loss, he didn't go and work for someone else, even though he was broke. He relied on no one else.

He relied on his own knowledge, experience and what Allah had given him. He knew how to negotiate, buy and sell, deal with people and find opportunities.

So even if you lose your money, you never lose your experience.

That's why you as an entrepreneur should go ahead and take calculated risks. Make it happen! If it doesn't, learn from it, that's all. Abdelrahman Ibn Auf along with many sahabi lost all their money. This has happened to multiple Muslims multiple times throughout history. I just told you the story of Mujeeb Ur Rahman and Yaya Ndianor. The key to success in the face of challenges is persistence. Whoever persists, will win in the long run.

LAUGH IT OFF

The prophet SAW said a believer is not bitten twice on the same spot. A believer cannot be fooled twice over the same mistake. This is a strong encouragement to avoid being naïve.

To avoid making the same mistake twice is to know who the enemy is. The enemy from within is Satan (Shaitan), who distracts us, he makes us forget things and makes us lazy.

So you have to know what your own character is like. If you start something and fail, be honest and ask yourself, "why did I really fail? Why didn't I succeed?"

Yes, there is destiny (Qadr), but analyse the situation further. Is it because you stopped working hard? Is it because of a lack of resources? Is it because of a lack of knowledge? If so, here is a resource in your hand now. Advice from Muslim Entrepreneurs that are tremendously successful. You will have the opportunity to contact some of them for coaching and advice. Remember, mistakes are lessons if you learn from them.

By accepting your mistakes, you will learn not to take yourself too seriously. Whenever you do something, it may work, it may not. Just do it with belief in Allah that He will give you what you need without taking it too seriously. The outcome isn't dependent on you if you prepare the right way. Ultimately, His promise for the believer is that you will be successful, either in this life or the next. So go forward with it. Taking yourself too seriously will only give you tremendous stress.

According to Imam Ashraf Zaghloul, CEO of NTG Clarity, a lot of people have ideas; entrepreneurs like to dream a lot, and they tend to be overprotective of their ideas. But at the end of the day, it is not the idea that counts. It's how you execute it and how much experience you have and how skilled you are. Funding is a big part as well.

So just go out there and do it. Don't try holding onto your so-called secret. It will make your enterprise fail. Instead, what is smart is to share your idea with everyone you meet with enthusiasm. Share it and see what happens. Read the chapter on the "Power of The Group", where I talk about how to surround yourself with people that will help you.

Now another step in not taking yourself too seriously is to actually aim for the "NO"; to go in expecting failure. So when you make a sale, go for the no and don't take it seriously.

They are not saying no to you, they're saying no to the sale. They are not ready to buy, their mindset may not be there, just move on without taking it too seriously and you will prosper that way. Fear of rejection is the reason a lot of people are scared of starting their own enterprises. Because being an entrepreneur involves making transactions and getting rejected and they unfortunately take themselves too seriously. They could be very successful are hindered by that fear.

I'll tell you about when I started going for the "NO" and what happened as a result. I was a graduate student and I wasn't making a lot of money. One of my karate friends told me that there was a company doing door-to-door sales. I had never sold anything at this point in English, because I was raised in Senegal and had always spoken French. But knocking on so many doors trying to get a sale changed that. It is the scariest thing out there. But once you do it, you realize you've been taking yourself too seriously. It just doesn't matter. Develop that attitude. Go for the "NO" sometimes. You'll get a yes eventually and you'll prosper. Again all you need is for some of the people to say yes some of the time for you to become successful beyond your imagination.

1% CAN MAKE YOU A MILLION

Whatever service you offer or whatever product you sell in your business, at the end of the day, it's how many sales you get that counts. The number of calls you make, the number of doors you ring and how many times you reach out to people. That is what matters.

In all these instances, you are vulnerable to rejection.

But if you realize that you do not need all of the people to say yes to you all of the time, that fear of rejection disappears. So remember: you do not need all of the people to say yes to you all of the time to become rich beyond your wildest imagination. All you need is for some of the people to say yes some of the time for you to become very, very rich.

For example, if today you live in Pakistan, there are 180 million people there, may Allah bless that country where a lot of the interviewees in this book are from. Now with 180 million people, lets just say 1% of those people buy your product. You might be selling chewing gum. If 1% of Pakistan buys your chewing gum, that's 1.8 million customers buying your brand! If you only make a dollar out of each person in that 1%, you're already a millionaire. If you gain more market share, you become a multimillionaire. See how fast your money can grow? So you don't need 100% of the population to say yes. Just some of the people some of the time. They don't have to buy from you all the time either. That is the attitude you must adopt and that is why persistence is key. Once you talk to enough people, some of them will say yes and buy your product. Eventually, you'll become rich.

So my assignment to you is this: make more calls, take more no's, and develop persistence.

Mujeeb Ur-Rahman told me another story of how he developed persistence. When he was a young man, he began working with his brother. They went to the Middle East and started working in construction. To begin with, they would just drive around town, spot building sites, and just go into the contractor's office.

There they would ask them, "what do you need?" The contractor may say cement, the amount they want and the time they require it by. They would make it their goal to provide that quantity by that time at the best price. And they developed a roll of a thousand customers like that within a few years. Very soon they were at the top of their game.

So just like that, from zero you can build a massive business by doing the groundwork yourself. They did it all by themselves by knocking on doors, talking to people and getting the customers.

2

THE IMPORTANCE OF HABITS

HABITS FORM CHARACTER

Character is your core being. It is how you really are when nobody is around, when you have no guests, wife or spouse around. You know yourself.

Now, how do we become the way we are? Some people get all the compliments; "this person is always working, they're always energetic, they're never late, they're so positive, they're so generous, they're so pious." How did they get that way? A lot of times, you'll see that they were not born that way. Some of the most tremendous entrepreneurs I met were just ordinary people that were failing to start with. They are different today.

Remember that a habit is something you do over and over again. When I was young, there was a boy I knew that was always stuttering. I used to hang out with him a lot and spend time with him. My parents didn't like it. I didn't understand why at the beginning. It wasn't just the stuttering, it was the fact that he was always playing instead of working. After spending so much time with him, I found myself stuttering one day too. It's amazing, you really learn it from the people around you. That is why it is so critical to have a good environment for you and your family; a good Islamic environment. You will always pick up the habits of people around you; be it in the workplace or society in general.

Just to get rid of that habit of stuttering took me some time. It really becomes a habit. You then have to work on stopping it becoming a part of you.

Later, I came across a study that was done into a tribe isolated from the rest of society. We mentioned this amazing story before. They had no stuttering in that entire tribe. They didn't even have a word to describe stuttering in their language. And nobody ever stuttered in that region. It goes to show, if you don't know about something, you will never do it, because it is not even in your vocabulary or field of vision.

That is a good reason why if you commit a sin, you should hide it and not expose it, talk about it or broadcast it, because you wouldn't want to influence people with your negative past.

How does this apply to you? I gave the example of stuttering, but really it applies to everything we do in this life. For example, thinking; you think the way you think because you've been thinking that way for some years now, and it becomes very difficult to change that unless you make an intentional effort. So thinking the right thoughts can become a habit.

The third step is that if you develop a habit, then that habit will change your priorities. So, if you are someone that is constantly thinking about bills and making ends meet, then that will be your reality. So, what you may tend to do is get the job that will just pay the bills because that is what a job will usually get you.

If you want to be an entrepreneur, then you must change your thinking. Instead of focusing on bills, focus on the opportunities around you, what you can do and the value you can provide society.
This will make you prosper tremendously, beyond just paying the bills.

A lot of entrepreneurs I talked to were far beyond just paying the bills. One of them is Salim Siddiqi, who became a multimillionaire just doing accounting, which is one of the hardest professions to do. You don't find a lot of accountants make it to the level he succeeded at, living in a million dollar house.

I can tell you that when he started out, he wasn't thinking about just making his bill payments. If he was, he wouldn't have quit the career he was already in, which was very well paid. But he left that security, worked hard from his basement and made it happen. There were nights he was literally sleeping on the floor with just a mattress, but look at where he is now. So you have to know that success is possible and accessible to you; it is just about thinking the right way.

THE LITTLE THINGS THAT COUNT

There is another myth out there, and it goes like this: "yeah those people persisted, yeah they were struggling, but all of a sudden they made it and became very rich."

No, it doesn't happen that way. You see, in this life there are laws that Allah has created. And for a farmer to reap his reward, he has to plant the seed first. That is why the first thing we said was have the right intention (Niyyah), plant your seed, and then you reap. Just like the farmer does.

Now how does this apply to you? It reminds you not to expect to become successful overnight. Sometimes it takes years. And that is why we talked about persistence, and the patience (sabr) that is required.

Nouman Ali Khan told me how he did a lot of work in the Arabic language and contributing to study of Quran, especially in the West, though now his organisation has gone global through the web.

He was emphasising the fact that when he first started his enterprise, he was already involved in teaching the Arabic language for years. It was only after the course became so popular that he decided to go into doing it full time. So, it wasn't something that happened overnight. Over that time, what was once a hobby became a life-long aspiration for him; that is to study and teach Arabic. Nowadays, he uses internet-marketing to build his business. He has close to a million subscribers on his channel, Bayyinah. tv. But all of that came later. He may be famous now, but that came after years of doing the work, sometimes even without seeing the results.

So, there is a myth out there that maybe some people just jump and reach the moon. It doesn't happen that way. Everyone goes through stages. My advice is just start small, do the tasks you need to produce results, and eventually you'll grow tremendously.

Another example of a small start up that grew exponentially is Dr. Yaqub Mirza's company, Amanah Mutual Funds. Dr. Mirza has been running his investment business for thirty years. So don't you think that after thirty years, he might know what he is doing? Of course! His persistence has paid off.

Dr. Hatim Zaghloul, founder of Wi-Lan Inc. likes to call it the myth of the overnight success. For seven years, he would work show up at the office at 6 in the morning long before any of his employees. Every single day. The gates of success opened up to him after 7 years of this kind of routine.

What do people see? Just the result: a billion dollar company. But they don't see the years of hard work that went into it.

So, rich people get rich by doing boring things. They tend to have the same routine day in and day out. You will find them involved in only one principal company and growing it. Even if they are investors, they will have areas of focus. Maybe they invest in many businesses, but primarily they are involved in one activity, in one niche, that they are known for. The marketplace is competitive enough to just make one enterprise work.

3

CHANGE YOUR HABITS

BUILD THAT MUSCLE

Start small. If you want to be healthy and lose weight, don't start with the marathon, you'll get sick! I knew a very young martial artist, who used to watch a martial arts movie, get excited and then he would go out and train really, really hard.

The result was obvious: he would feel pain all over his body! It was tough! But later on as he progressed, he became wiser about it, doing a little bit consistently every week. That is what you want to do.

Build your muscle. Whether in your business, personal life or marriage- don't throw just one big party. Do lots of small consistent ones.

Start small and work towards your goal. If you want to become a millionaire, become a "thousandaire" first, then a "ten-thousandaire" and "hundred-thousandaire". That is what I've seen from the most successful people.

They start small and remain very consistent. How consistent? Do it everyday. Islam teaches us this, and it is a tremendous benefit; consistency. The prophet SAW said:

"Upon you is that which you have the ability to do. By Allah, Allah will never become bored, and will thus continue to reward you until you yourself become bored with doing good deeds. Verily, the most beloved Deed to Allah is that which an individual is the most consistent upon."

- Al-Bukhaari, Vol. 1 Book 2 Hadith 41

So be consistent. It may be one of the hardest things to do, but it is the most rewarding. You will find as you build your muscle, it gets easier. Just like with your five daily prayers. When you first started, it seemed so difficult! But now, it's a part of life. That is how Islam teaches us consistency as a fundamental principle.

The richest people you meet are the most consistent. Every day, they work at the same time, do the same activity, do the same "boring" (in some people's minds) business. That makes them grow and grow and become successful. That is why one of the things that hampers a lot of people is jumping from one industry to another. But if you are consistent and do the same thing over and over again, you will become very good at it.

How long does it take to get into the good habit? Islamically, thirty days is a good number. Why do I say that? Because some scholars reminded me that when we fast in Ramadan, it is a thirty day period on average. Those thirty days you are fasting are supposed to change you deeply for the following eleven months of the year. You develop the habit of not eating too much. It helps bring health back into your life. It also gives us that persistence we need. So thirty days.

You want to break a habit? Maybe it is being late every day. Aim to be on time for just thirty days and see what happens. Everything is codified in this beautiful religion. Consistency; we do the same thing over and over again, at the same time, every day of the year. Look at salah, it is consistency; it is the same prayer every time. It is done the same way at the same time every day. So the habit of consistency is built in, which is why the Muslim entrepreneur has a tremendous advantage.

"IT'S BEEN YEARS SINCE I'VE BEEN LATE"

Where do bad habits come from? They are learnt. Even if it is a sin, it's learnt. The source could be as simple as TV. It's highly recommended to turn it off; every successful entrepreneur that I met hardly watches TV.

They're too busy either studying their faith or profession, or dreaming up the next big plan, building their business or their community. They're just too busy to watch TV. There are hardly any beneficial tips for entrepreneurship on TV. Learn good things from good people. Stay within a positive environment. Go and ask! Successful Muslim Entrepreneurs are the most open people I've ever met. You too will find them to be so happy to share the wisdom they accumulated over years of experience that you might not have. You can learn from their wisdom. Truly, I am grateful for the opportunity to have learnt extensively from them.

So where else does a bad habit come from? Another source is riyah; showing off. For example, to do something simply to look cool. You will hardly find a "cool" rich person. Sure they have fans, but they tend to have enemies too. It comes with the success. And they're not afraid of that. Especially Muslim Entrepreneurs, because they are the most down-to-earth. They especially are not trying to show off. Thus, if you are right now in a career just because you want to look good, it will be very difficult for you to become truly successful.

You see, the successful entrepreneur is willing to even sell peanuts to make it. Aliko Dangote's grandfather became wealthy selling groundnuts in Nigeria. Now you may think groundnut is really insignificant, but he became the wealthiest man in his country just from selling those nuts. This is what you have to understand; the richest entrepreneurs out there are willing to do what they have to do (as long as it's legal)!

This characteristic is praised in the Quran, and is highly beneficial. These people are not working to show off. They are not working to look good.

Therefore, don't develop a bad habit of showing off; it really hampers not only your business, but your life and happiness. It can be something that can happen to any of us. So re-read the section on 'Intentions'.

Reconnect with your 'why'. Why are you doing what you are doing? If it isn't to look good, then what is it really for? I've been advised many times by entrepreneurs I interviewed to review my intentions and to reconnect with my 'why'.

Thirdly, the Devil (Shaytaan) belittles a bad habit. He makes it out like it isn't a big deal, so you keep repeating it. Like being late; if it's just a party you're late to, it may be OK, but one day it may be something important, and it will affect your business.

Let's say a contractor gave you an order for building materials, but you brought his shipment in late. That will just make him move on and become someone else's customer, and you can lose a great opportunity. So do not belittle bad habits. Be conscious of that. Take everything that is bad as a big deal. I met a billionaire once that told me he was never late to any appointment. We were in a hotel meeting, talking about his routine, and he told me "you know what, Oumar? It's been years since I've been late." And it's true, at every meeting, he would be the first person there. Even though he was by far the most successful out of all of us; he was already a billionaire! People were coming to see him, yet he was always there first, ahead of time, before they were.

So, next time you hear people say: "that person is rich just because that's how it is." Say, no. Remind yourself that they have some of the right virtues. It isn't the evil person that wins.

Successful people have certain virtues. Don't belittle your bad habits; take them seriously so you can amend them and you too will rise to the top.

KNOW YOUR ENEMY

Identify the bad habit; know the enemy first. Then get rid of it. How? By replacing it with a good habit.

One of the many great resources of the Muslim Entrepreneur is the Sunnah. The Quran didn't just come down by itself. It came with the messenger SAW who was a walking example of the Quran. He truly exemplified all of the virtues Allah loves in life, in business, in everything. So follow the Sunnah.

If the prophet SAW did something, it is a good habit to have. That is good enough to repeat it. If we know he didn't sleep too much, then you take that on board. He would wake up at night. You think that will make you healthier? Absolutely! It is very difficult to be too chubby if you stand up for a few hours every night. He would always be riding and walking in harsh desert conditions. Today, we may not have horseback or camel, but we can replicate it with exercise. Everything in his Sunnah is a good habit. That is what the Muslim Entrepreneurs told me, too.

Whilst speaking with Dr. Noor, CEO of Noor Khan Hospital in Hafr Al-Batin, Saudi Arabia, I asked him: "what do you read to become successful?" He told me he reads the Quran and he follows the way of the prophet SAW.

Dr. Noor's service has been so exemplary that he is one of the few foreign nationals in Saudi Arabia issued with honorary citizenship rights by the King of Saudi Arabia himself. But he made it happen because of the tremendous work he has done for that country; the services he has provided, the contribution he has made to them. He was recognised for that. At 80 years old, he is still building his business. He goes to work every single day. And reads the Quran daily. There is no stopping a true entrepreneur.

So follow the Sunnah when it comes to building good habits and you will be successful.

THE MONEY HABIT

Saving is a habit, investing is a habit, and wasting the money is also a habit. So if you do something often enough, you will develop that habit. This book is about money. When you implement what is in it and form these good habits, you will grow tremendously rich insha'Allah.

So how do you get good money-handling habits? There are many examples of how to do this from the Quran. Allah doesn't like spend-thrifts; He calls them the brothers of the devils, because they don't control their desires.

You want to grow your purse? Leave your money in the purse. You see that beautiful dress? Leave it- don't buy it. You want to eat chocolate? You want to buy delicious chicken? Refrain. Fasting teaches us this.

Don't try to keep up with your rich neighbours Abdullah and Fatima. If your neighbours have built another floor on top of their house or bought a new Lexus, it will be difficult for you to save and grow money if you try competing with them. Forget about impressing others. Read this book. Distribute it. Learn about money. If you apply this information, you can rest assured that you will be financially independent in a few years while your neighbours are paying their debt. For now, your only competition is yourself!

One good rule of thumb is to keep a percentage between 10% and 25% of everything you earn. And allow that money to grow through your investments.

Dr. Noor of Saudi Arabia told me he saves his money. That is one of the key principles of his success. Of course, he is no miser, either. He treats his family very well and looks after all of his children and grandchildren, gives them gifts and a good, prosperous life. But he never spends the money he makes on useless things. Especially whilst he was starting out and growing his business.

So start as early as possible. If you want to invest, then you have to give your money time to grow. It's a good practice to start as early as possible. If you're in your twenties, you should have already started.

THE DEATH OF T.V.

Just listen to yourself. Are you discouraging yourself without realizing it?

Are you speaking negatively about yourself and the goals and dreams you haven't achieved yet? Are you bogged down by insecurities at work?

Listen to yourself. If people are talking negatively around you, leave. This is an instruction from the Quran; to avoid useless speech (laghw) that is not beneficial in this life or the next. Just avoid it; leave. Avoid TV and whatever is a waste of time on social media for the same reason. If it is useless, then you don't need to know it. Avoid that negativity.

The second step is to avoid being lazy with your language. Express what you want in a clear way so there is no conflict between your goals, dreams and current reality. Remember, Allah provides for us through other people. So whilst making a sale or doing a deal, speak in a clear way. How can you do that? By listening to good things. Listen to audios and people that know how to speak. Listen to rich people and speak to them; note how they speak. Through this book, you will access the audio and video recordings of interviews from the people that are featured here. This is a great resource to start learning how to speak well.

So how does one develop the language of rich thinking? Not only should you listen to wealthy Muslims, but keep their company too. Ask them for good advice (naseeha) so you can interact with them consistently. It will make you grow.

POWER OF DHIKR

Dhikr is something very special in Islam; our lips are constantly moving in Allah's remembrance. Whether you are getting into your car, working, getting out of bed, eating, greeting guests or praying in all those moments our lips are constantly moving in remembrance of Allah.

So constantly remember Allah. That is the power of dhikr. He is our Lord that is providing for us. When you have that constant reminder, it is very difficult to have fear or confusion in your decision making. If you find yourself stressed whilst working towards your goals and dreams, remember Allah.

Du'a has the same power. You are constantly in contact with the One who provides and everything is in His power. Arif Mirza told me, "one thing we don't have in common with non-Muslims is that they believe their success is because of them, how hard they worked and so on." But the Muslim Entrepreneurs know their success isn't just from them. They attribute it first and foremost to Allah, and then maybe their parents and their families. You'll see Muslim Entrepreneurs have a very close relationship with their families and especially their parents. You'll see them helping them and praising them a lot.

One of the things I noticed in Mr Siddiqi is his tremendous love for his father. He remembers waking up at night seeing him pray. And his father was a businessman.

That gave him the vision and role model he needed to become a businessman himself. I could really see the love he has for his parents. He had a great amount of humbleness and awe whilst praising his father; how he remembered him to be very calm, focused, intelligent and sharp.

Now, what does that tell you? Success is not just because of what we are and what we achieve. What we are is a result of what our parents gave us; the love, education and religion they gave us. There is that balance that the Muslim Entrepreneur has that I haven't seen in anyone else.

PRINCIPLE IX

CRITICAL SKILLS

1

BEING COACHABLE

FIBONACCI'S TEACHER

We'll discuss two kinds of "education"; theoretical and practical. Firstly, there is practical education. It's informal and known as being 'Street Smart'. You can get this by starting your own business.

So to get a schooling in practical education, start your enterprise as soon as possible. Do something small. Turn your hobby into a business. But get that informal knowledge and learn how to start, even at a small scale. While I was in high school, I used to make my money by selling comic books. It was very profitable. Then I went into selling mathematical text books. That was very profitable, too. It was quick money; and helped me to learn those skills. This kind of experience can serve you tremendously in your business dealings.

Then there is the knowledge you get in school, which can be useful as well. In the Islamic tradition, knowledge has always been a key resource for traders and religious people alike.

Religious knowledge is not just the knowledge of religious rulings. The knowledge you get in school can be important and religious too if used the right way. For example, it's known that someone like Leonardo Fibonacci, the famous Italian Mathematician from the 13th century, introduced algebra and equation based systems into the West. But where did he get his education? From the Islamic centres of learning in Algeria, which was a lively, bustling trading port at the time. Fibonacci's father was a tradesman who used to visit Algeria often to trade. He learnt his algebra from there and brought it over to Europe. That is how today we are still making use of Fibonacci numbers. As a mathematician, I learnt them in the first year of university. So business and knowledge are tied together in the Islamic learning system. After all, the two centres of any Muslim city are the Masajid (mosques) and the Souks (markets).

For this reason, reading and writing have always been very important to Muslims. They are fundamental for trade. These skills were needed to put contracts into writing.

Remember: the scope of theoretical knowledge may be limited. Practical knowledge will help you more in the long run. But it doesn't hurt to get both.

HOW TO BE COACHABLE

Be open. The first step is to be open to receive that coaching. In Islam, once you really ask for help, first and foremost from Allah; that is where humility comes in.

Being coachable is to admit that you don't know. Sometimes, you really don't know what you don't know; meaning you may think you know something but once you start exploring it, you realize you don't. Say I want to start selling houses; and I think it's easy, but I've never done it before, so I don't really know. I don't even know what I need to know to be successful. That is where you need a mentor that will guide you through the steps of success. We talked about mentorship earlier on.

Have the courage to ask. The Quran says to keep humility. "Don't walk upon the earth in a state of haughtiness", rather be humble, because you cannot pass the mountains or split the earth.

That is what you will see from the practice of the prophet SAW. Whatever he did, he would consult his companions first, whether it is an expedition or something that involves the community, he would ask for advice. Even in family matters, like when his wife was accused of adultery, he asked for advice. Asking is a sign of strength of character. It is a sign of integrity, that the person has nothing to hide, and the prophet SAW's life was very open. When working as an entrepreneur and as a community leader, you want to ask people working for you as well as people with more experience than you. Allah says to ask people that know more than you if you don't know.

That is one of the things that motivated me to write this book. I myself did not know how some Muslim Entrepreneurs became so tremendously successful; they became such big leaders in their communities. So since I didn't know, I asked. And this book is the response they gave me.

SHARPEN YOUR SWORD

As an entrepreneur, you need experience. Sometimes, it is wise to have someone that will show you the way. You want to choose the right employer for that and have the right intention. You want to learn the ropes of the business before going on your own.

Many entrepreneurs I interviewed started off being employees themselves first. They became successful in their own right at a later stage of their life.

You see, you really are not competing with anyone. You are competing only with your own self. You are competing with your own personal best self. If you have that right intention, then you can find the people that will help you the most. That is the right type of company. A company that is nurturing and will allow you to develop your skills.

Dr. Mirza started off teaching and doing different forms of work. Mujeeb Ur-Rahman started out by working for his father. Many were already in family businesses, which helped them go into their own businesses directly. Even if they worked for their fathers and grandfathers, the point is they worked for someone else.

So, if you want to learn how to sell, then just work for someone that is selling right now. That is how you will learn the skill.

Aliko Dangote, the richest man in all of Africa, if not the richest Muslim, was quoted saying that he learnt tremendously from his maternal grandfather, the richest man in Nigeria. Now what does that tell you? It tells you something about business skill. That we are not born into these skills, but we develop them.

So you have to be a smart employee. Like most people, you too may want to get a job for finances; to save up before you can start on your own. Whatever your reason, choose someone that will nurture and develop your skill. Even if it is a smaller firm, you can learn hands on how to invest, grow a company and work efficiently. Later on these skills will come in handy afterwards when you go into business on your own.

WHY HE'S BUYING ARSENAL

Dr. Abdullah Idris Ali, of Sudanese origin, is a man that is tremendous in dealing with people. He is always smiling, despite running a lot of affiliated businesses and even a school alongside his organisation. He is the president of ISNA Canada, the biggest Muslim organisation in the region. Through ISNA, Dr. Ali deals with the general public, the authorities, investors and of course his Muslim community.

What he practices is inspired by the Prophet SAW's character. He deals with young and old alike whilst being very accessible. This is despite his position and responsibility. To lead your business, you too must learn this skill, because at the end of the day, as a business leader you want to inspire the people working with you to take on the right activities and actions.

Secondly, if you want to inspire the customer to take action and buy your product or service, then sell your company like a big brand.

One of the things Aliko Dangote does well is this. With a personal net worth of over $20 billion, Aliko has made a brand for himself. What is he associated with? Wealth, success and business. The Dangote name is associated with Wealth in all of Africa. Everything you will see them do is geared towards this brand building. When they take a decision, it is a strong decision and people can trust in it. He is even in the process of buying the famous English football club Arsenal FC. This is to showcase Nigeria's economic success worldwide.

Remember; customers, government, investors - all want familiarity. They don't want a stranger they don't know. Branding creates this familiarity. If your reputation is not good, not only will you lose your customers but they won't give you the referrals you need. Yet, if you have a strong name, people will come back again and again.

We see this all the time with successful designer brands. People are willing to pay the price for good brands. A person will buy a BMW just because it is known to be one of the best cars. Branding is a key exercise in inspiring people.

2

CORE BUSINESS SKILLS

SPECIALIZE

Knowledge is key for a successful enterprise. You can have specialised knowledge or general knowledge. Now, you'll want to develop special knowledge that will allow you to be an expert and master what you do.

If you are providing a service, whether accounting or selling homes, use the real-life examples in this book to remind yourself that you can be rich doing pretty much anything. As long as you do the job well, with a high level of professionalism and set it up the right way.

Dr. Ike Ahmed, one of the best eye specialists in the world, exemplifies this principle. Still in his 30's, he is leading the way in the surgical management of glaucoma. This is a very niche area of expertise, yet it brings in over $6 billion annually for the medical industry he is a part of.

It is after all the second biggest cause of blindness worldwide. Dr. Ike has discovered that the traditional use of eye-drops and surgery are not a good enough cure; and is spearheading an alternative treatment.

So what you see in most successful people is that they specialize in one area. You stay in that area until you master it. It can take years of experience, but it will be worth it.

That's why I've often seen entrepreneurs turn their hobbies into opportunities. They do what they love and it's easier that way for them to commit to that activity. Now you too can do the same.

One of my interviewees, Dr. Zahoor Qureshi, enjoyed making and selling greeting cards; something he had learnt from his father. This hobby eventually turned into a million-dollar fulltime business. That goes to show you really can build something tremendous just out of a hobby. Dr. Zahoor's business made him good money from the beginning; because of his passion for it. He even gave up his daytime job (though very well paid) later on to run the business fulltime and that allowed him to make much more. He realized you can never earn as much when working for other people.

YOUR FIRST RESOURCE

As an entrepreneur, you'll be dealing with people constantly, whether as customers, employers, employees, investors, family members or society in general. You're constantly dealing with people.

One of the things I've seen in exceptional Muslim business and community leaders is they use the skills they've learnt in their leadership roles to prosper. They're really good at forging relationships, for example.

In the case of Mr. Nazir Ahmed, his technique isn't getting into investment clubs. Those are good for beginner entrepreneurs to get contacts, but in the long run, personal contacts are everything. You have to know the people you work with on a personal level. Visit these people so you can gain their trust and do good business with them. Long term relationships are for winners.

Nazir Ahmed is always favouring personal connections. He is sitting on the board of many companies, which allows him to help multinational firms expand by putting the right people in front of them. He does it well because he knows his people. Those kinds of relationships however develop over a period of several years through personal contacts. So develop your personal contacts.

Another way to develop people skills is by developing your company culture.

Take the example of Mrs. Oumou Ndiaye, a very successful founder of a customs management software company in Senegal. Her approach to people is to make them take ownership of the company. Every time she sees even the cleaning lady, she wants to make sure she feels like the company is her own. That makes the employee feel special and feel a sense of real belonging to the company.

Company culture is everything. If your company culture is negative and exploitative, it's not something you want to be a part of long term.

So as an entrepreneur, create a culture in your company that encourages thriving. One example that Mr. Rizvee gave me was of how he chooses his employees. He would interview a person several times, putting them through test scenarios, just to test how they react and how they make decisions. For him, those things are very important. It's not uncommon for him to go through at least twenty or more applicants just to find the right one. That is because he appreciates how important it is to know the people you work with. They are your first resource. They are the most important.

People talk about investment and money, but really the best resource is human capital. You must treat them well to prosper. Allow your people to grow, and make use of their creativity within the parameters of your company. You will prosper tremendously this way.

THE HOME-OFFICE

Learn the skill of growing your money and growing your business. Anything you don't know about this, learn it.

One way is to invest in the society around you. I've learnt this from many of the entrepreneurs I interviewed, including Dr. Athar Khatib. He started his own business from his living room with his wife.

They now run a thriving clinic. His list of clientele includes the Sultan of Brunei. That is how renowned his service is as a leading eye-surgeon. Yet, despite his busy schedule, he takes the time to regularly hold award ceremonies for high school graduates at his local masjid. He does this to reward their achievements and encourage his community.

Now, you too want to help your community, especially those that are poor. This is a big exhortation in Islam. Help the people that are in need. Allah has promised you will be paid back for giving in His cause in both this life as well as the next.

Secondly, you have to understand the highest return on your investment is to run your own business; bar none. Not the bank, or someone else. It is just you as an entrepreneur. So you have to believe in your product and move forward with it. When the money comes, reinvest it so that you grow faster. It is very important to reinvest your money, because a lot of people fail in business if their funds run out and they can't find an investor.

Thirdly, it is very important that you keep operational costs low. As you saw from these stories, some Muslim Entrepreneurs saved by simply starting their business in a basement. How much do you think that cost them? To start a business in their own basement, and use their own home phone, and their own self as an employee. It costs next to nothing to start a business like that. Remember, money management is very important in order to grow.

Dr. Miles Davis, a professor in Entrepreneurship and dean of a great business school, confirmed with his research that many businesses fail because the money isn't there. The investment wasn't there.

So either you have enough funds, or you start the business in a way that minimises your expenses. Do it yourself without hiring. Do what you have to do to grow the business yourself first.

FRANCHISE

It's not just about getting the business started. It's also getting the right structure.

Don't over-hire when you first start. Just meet the needs of the market. Don't follow blindly what others are doing. Like getting a lot of employees with fancy uniforms before you can afford their payroll! Instead, focus on where the money is and invest in that activity.

It also requires a lot of humility to say, 'hey, you know what, I have a house, I'll just start it from there without using a fancy office.'

At the end of the day, a business is not about how you look or what fancy car you're driving. Of course, appearance is good, remain presentable, but it's not just about the glitter. It's the content. What the customer cares about at the end of the day is service.

For example, Mr. Rizvee was driving a Toyota Corolla even while he was making millions of sales. Even after two years of starting a multi-million-dollar enterprise, he kept humble in his Corolla.

When I met Com Mirza, I had my suit and shiny boots on.

But the multi-millionaire 33-year old turned up in a polo-neck shirt, also driving a Corolla. He reassured me later on that his Rolls-Royce is parked in his garage under the Burj Khalifa in Dubai.

Now lets go back to learning about how to structure correctly. You have to be willing to release control.

One of the things Mr. Rizvee asked me to consider was this:

"How many people can I really micromanage in a day?"

- Azim Rizvee, CEO Minmaxx Realty Inc.

Not that many, right? Just one person. So at the end of the day, you have to trust your employees. You can't control every activity they do. You can instead leverage some level of control by hiring the right type of people, get the right type of contacts, and then go from there.

Mr. Rizvee's business model is to allow his employees to become entrepreneurs themselves. He lets them run their own sales locations. He benefits tremendously that way. By allowing the employee to become an entrepreneur in their own right, he runs his business almost like a franchise. That is a strategy you will also see in network marketing; which also makes use of the franchise system technique.

DO THE RIGHT THING

When you are running your enterprise, you want to focus on things that bring in the most value.

We talked about how selling is everything; it's where the money is. If no product or service is sold, then there is no value in your company. So focus most of your time on activity that produces income.

Now, to go to the next level, when you're faced with decision making as a business owner, you will at times have tough decisions to make. You have to ask yourself; how does it feel? If it feels good for the company and for you, and it feels good morally, meaning Islamically, then it's the right thing to do. If it is also in the best interest of your family - then go forward. That is how you make a decision. And once you decide to go forward, don't turn back. Just trust in Allah. You will see success. This is what I learnt from Mr. Rizvee too: "just know that this is the right thing to do and do it". People will be judged by their actions after all, not just their talk.

Remember that by taking massive action, you can really create a movement. For example, there is a concept out there that to do business, you need an office and a nice car. No, neither is essential to do business. Business is just the transaction between you and the client. There is no need for an office. You can have one later on, once you grow. So focus on the important thing, which is the customer.

For example, I learnt from Zahoor Qureshi never to compromise on quality. Whilst setting up his hobby-craft business, if his product had even the slightest deficiency he would kill the line. He wouldn't bring the product to the market because it would ruin his reputation. Besides, it's not the right thing to do. He invested in the best designers, ones that worked for international brands, and commissioned only the best ideas. Like Mr. Nazir Ahmed says:

"You have to be honest."

- Nazir Ahmed, House of lords, UK

Never over-promise. What you put out there will come back to you, multiplied. You reap what you sow; good or bad. An example of Nazir reaping the good he sowed is when he told one of his clients exactly what he would get before the transaction. His client was a Sikh customer who came to him wanting to purchase a shop. Mr. Nazir knew the shop was doing a turn-over of close to £15,000 a month. Yet, he told his client the shop was doing around £7,000, keeping it conservative. The man came back and said to him, "wow this shop is doing way over £10,000!" So he was happy to do the transaction because he didn't feel cheated. He was given a figure on the modest side of what the site was actually producing, so once he discovered the real value was surplus of what he was quoted, it made him even more satisfied.

It's not just talk, but it's in action. People will get rich if they do the right thing. If you cheat on your customer, they won't come back. Consider long term decisions that provide the maximum quality of service in order to prosper.

3

KNOW YOUR CUSTOMER

MONEY FROM THIN-AIR

Selling has been mentioned in the Quran. It really is one of the very few professions that has been mentioned explicitly. Allah says He has made selling allowed. That is a strong exhortation for going into business as a Muslim Entrepreneur.

It's also known that selling brings in the money. Either from a customer, another business or the stock market. Whatever it may be, selling requires some kind of transfer of money. So it makes sense to learn to sell and negotiate.

Dr. Mirza told me that he learnt the art of selling from his grandfather and his father. A key component of what he learnt about how to sell was the art of negotiating.

When you talk to a potential investor like in Dr. Mirza's line of business, it's all about selling on your competence to preserve their capital and to deliver great results on your investments.

Selling is really the gateway to success in any enterprise. You'll find some of the highest paid professionals are actually salespeople.

Who do you think makes the most money; the doctor that does the surgery, extremely specialized in their field, or the salesman who sells the expensive machines the hospital uses? You guessed it; the salesman makes double what the doctor makes, if not more.
So who do companies value the most? A good salesperson. That's you as a business owner. Once you learn how to sell, you will prosper.

That is the profession of the prophet SAW, too. He sold in his early years. There is an Islamic tradition that says 90% of your rizq comes through trade. This is entrepreneurship. If you want to become rich; sell!

Understand that as an individual, you are constantly selling. Even when you are working for someone else in the beginning, you are selling on your skills. You have to convince the business owner that their time and money are well spent on employing you. Taking you on is not charity; it's selling. You are selling your skills.

If you are a father or a mother, you're "selling" good behaviour and morals to your children, teaching them to keep up their salawat and so on. The job of a good parent is convincing their child to do good for themselves. So it's a critical component to success in many aspects of life. You have to be compelling and convincing.

That's why I found most business leaders to be very compelling whilst discussing their company vision with me. Sometimes I even wanted to buy into their business right away because they convey what they're doing so well! They make it so appealing. So learn how to sell. How do you learn? By practice.

START MARKETING

You're always engaged in marketing. Market yourself; we covered that previously. Also learn to market your business, market your product in the best possible way. Learn the best practices in the market place.

It starts with yourself. Get a good self-image. I remember interviewing the owner of REDCO, Mr. Mujeeb Ur Rahman. One of the things he stressed was how a person should take good care of themselves; value presenting themselves well and dress well. This is something I saw in all of the Muslim Entrepreneurs I interviewed. They take good care of themselves. That's also from the sunnah of the prophet SAW. If you have the means, then show it through your lifestyle.

Sheikh Said Rageah told me that one of the principles of Islam is to be grateful to Allah. So if you are successful and financially comfortable, show it outwardly. This is part of being grateful to Allah for the blessings He has given you.

It also lets other people know that you're doing well, so if they need your help they can ask you. It's therefore highly discouraged to hide the favours you have been blessed with.

One of the best ways to learn about marketing and image making is by travelling. Learn from other people. Allah says,

"O mankind, indeed We have created you from male and female and made you peoples and tribes that you may know one another. Indeed, the most noble of you in the sight of Allah is the most righteous of you. Indeed, Allah is Knowing and Acquainted."

- Al-Quran, Surah Al-Hujurat, Ayah 13

That is strong encouragement for us to go out there and learn from other people. That is what the sahaba did. And that is why, to this day you'll see Muslim Entrepreneurs migrating from Asia to the Middle East, or from America to East Africa and Australia, away from their native country, travelling all over the world and building what they have to build. They are learning from the experiences of the people around them.

In the past, Muslims have learnt from leaders of all kinds of societies. Hindu traditions, Greeks, Ethiopians, Persians and Europeans.
They learnt from them all and enriched our civilisation a lot. Many good things come from travelling the world.

Mr. Rizvee told me sometimes he goes out there and travels to learn how to give the best experience he can to a customer.
The customer is the end goal; you want to give them the best experience they can have.

To learn about quality customer service, Mr. Rizvee went to Dubai and stayed at the world's only seven star hotel. When his child got injured there, they had to call a doctor, which the hotel did for them. The doctor came all the way to their suite, treated the child on the spot, and they were able to get on with their day without paying any charges. For a similar doctor's call in a five-star hotel in Switzerland, he had to pay an extra 500 euros. That is the difference between a seven-star hotel in Dubai and a 5 star hotel in Europe; one simply provides a far superior level of service. It is a world-class standard of service.

That is what you want to do for your business. Give your customer the best experience possible; it will make it easier for them to buy! Remember, for them to give you their money, you have to give them more value than the rest of the marketplace.

CAN YOU RELATE?

For commercial reasons, get to know what the customer needs. Lets talk about the Islamic perspective on this. Throughout history, you'll see the best traders identify customer needs before they do the transaction. This is how you make a big fortune. For you, whether you're working on the internet or trading in commodities, just identify what your customer needs, and then fulfil that need. As entrepreneurs, all we do is transfer value into the marketplace. That is why it is wise to say the client comes first.

Again from Azim Rizvee, we learn that you have to treat every customer like they will be the last customer you'll have. Treat them like kings and queens. Give them maximum value.

Why?

Because that customer is not just one customer. They could equate a hundred customers for you over a lifetime. What could happen is that one satisfied customer could refer you to two others, who refer you to five more, and so on. This can lead to exponential growth; and over a lifetime they could keep buying from you.

Let's say a top-class real estate broker like Mr. Rizvee is able to satisfy his customer with his new house. Now, they will keep coming back and doing business with him. It's not a onetime shot, where you just hit and run. You have to provide value so that people can come back to you again.

Now, that gives you a strong incentive as a business owner to follow up with your customer. That is what the best winners do. You don't just make a sale. You make a sale, then follow up with the customer to make sure he is happy. You provide more service. You give them your best product and let them know what the latest is in availability that matches their criteria. In this way, you are constantly engaging with them. Read more on marketing to learn how to do this well.

It's also important to realize that selling is a transfer of belief. That is why it is so good when you relate to your prospect. If you believe your product is good, you believe that your customer needs it, and then you provide that service, you get a happy customer.

What you've essentially done is transfer the belief; that belief enables the exchange of a product for money. You have to consider all of this in order to make the transaction successful.

NO GAMBLING

"Don't gamble, OK? Just don't gamble!"

I heard about the dangers of gambling from Dr. Yaqub Mirza, who doesn't invest in things he doesn't know. He is not the kind of investor that is always risking his capital. He is using sound investment techniques after studying the fundamentals of the businesses he is investing in.

What he does is pool the money from investors and make commissions from it. He is making a tremendous job out of this tactic. His investments grew by over 13% per year in the past 10 years; This performance beats almost all of his competition in terms of growth.

One of the things he is also good at is buying businesses. He goes out there and negotiates with business owners before buying from them.

The kind of experience Dr. Mirza has is learnt from doing, not just theory. Yet the school system teaches just that; only theory. In that sense, it has failed most people that want to be entrepreneurs.

What was supposed to give us opportunity and open-mindedness has brought in conformity and people working in a system that is already established. Schooling teaches us to be risk averse, instead of teaching calculated risk taking.

In the words of Mr. Rizvee, "you shouldn't be bribed". That is what employment is; work for someone else through bribery; being bribed into doing someone else's work for temporal economic benefit. Yet that doesn't build you lasting wealth. You'll see a lot of people using banks for their savings, but your own enterprise is where your money will grow the fastest. To escape that bribery, take calculated risks to establish your own institutions.

Technology is here to help. The internet has made the world really flat, you can build a business pretty much everywhere. That is a tremendous, open opportunity. If you look at the education system right now; schools like Harvard, increasingly so, are creating business builders and leaders. In every field, from military to industry to journalism, leaders of society that create institutions are being manufactured. All the institutions you see around you were created by someone after all, and we can do the same. We just have to have the vision, the work ethics, and see the opportunity where it is, to really create a movement within our respective industries and communities.

In the same way, you'll find that most big institutions like universities will have endowment funds, sometimes in the billions; but what do they use it for?

They put it in a bank to keep it safe. Islam does not condone that; it condones risk taking, calculated risk taking where you know what you are doing.

This may mean the rich may become not so rich, and the poor can become rich. But at least opportunity stays open for everybody. That is how Islam provides a better way for someone looking to create a fortune for themselves.

WEALTH BUILDING STRATEGIES

1

WISDOM WITH MONEY

CREATE MORE STREAMS OF INCOME

In modern societies, 90% of people have active income. That means they go, get an education or learn a certain skill, apply to work for a company, and then get paid; monthly, weekly, and so on. You get paid a fraction of your production based on how much time you put in. That's the most popular form of earning income. It's active income. People work; sometimes from 25 to 65 if not more nowadays, given people are living longer.

The second way of earning money is business income. This is split into two; the first is actively engaging in the business. Here, you're putting in your own labour and getting paid by your customers or by other businesses.

Somehow , you are getting paid by putting in the hours. An example would be a salon or restaurant or accounting business, where owners use their skills and education to provide services in exchange for active income. It's active, but it's also business. You can grow very wealthy doing that. Now you're dealing directly with the client and if you structure your business properly, you could build enough revenue using systems where per hour you're making more than someone else makes in a day. A lot of the entrepreneurs I interviewed became millionaires that way. That is active business income.

The third type of income is an income that may at first sound like a dream. It's an income where you don't have to work at all. It's called residual income.

When people take on creative activities, like writing books, or producing an artistic product that they sell; be it a record or a sculpture, they earn residually. Residual income is how landlords that employ property management companies do. That is what people that have patents do. They get a patent, and then they let other people use their patent. They don't have to do anything after that for twenty, thirty, fifty years. That's a dream income.

Make sure that by the time you retire, your residual income is stronger than your active income. It's important because our bodies are finite, we can get sick. We get old. We just have a given amount of days to work in a year. So make your residual income as strong as possible. That's what we'll be talking about here.

Now, is this kind of income a new concept? You see, at least 90% of people have jobs nowadays, even among Muslims. It's a global phenomenon.

Yet, it was different before. People had sheep, cows and fields. Tangible assets like land, minerals, trade and weaponry meant people were secure.

Yet, nowadays, most people are taught to have jobs in order to be secure. So, the main source of income is active, working income. The highest of which may be some professional position. This may be a doctor or a lawyer getting a big salary. Some people may get rich that way, but they have to put in typically a very high number of hours.

Now, if you really want to work smart, then build wealth by upping your residual income. If you go into business, think about how to make your business residual so you don't have to work eighty hours per week for forty years.

Most people work that way, expecting a return and some security when they get retired. Then at the time of retirement, their income is cut by half, or they are only left with 40% of what their pre-retirement income after inflation.

Therefore, think residual. It's the first step to getting wealthy.

Residual wealth is not new to Islamic societies. In Islam, Allah talks about wealth alongside children. That is because the main type of residual income people had before was their children. So you would get married in your teens, have your children, and by the time people were in their forties, they had a generation ready to replace them and do the work, so they could relax.

Nowadays, that model doesn't seem to be true anymore because people are having fewer children and marrying later.

That is why the term residual income is very popular. Instead of the income coming in through traditional means, people must work for it themselves.

Thus, what you can do is set up a business that has some kind of residual income attached to it, or patent something, write something, create something. Just work on the residual part of business building.

A good example would be parking spaces. If you buy something like that; then year after year, you're just collecting people's fees.

Think about other ways of making residual income. There are many. It's one of the big ways to become very wealthy.

SAVE, SAVE, SAVE

Saving is really the first step to grow wealth. If you don't have the habit of saving then there is no greatness in you.

Salim Siddiqi gave a piece of advice to the Muslim Entrepreneur or to anybody looking to build lasting success: "you need to live within your means. Allah does not love spendthrifts."

Build your business first. Use your money to build your business. Then you can get all the furniture you want! When he was building his business, he bought an unfurnished house and slept on the floor. He lived that way for three or four years.

They now live in a beautiful multi-million dollar mansion, MashaAllah!

The habit of saving; that's how you win big in business. Now how much should you be saving? Most of the people of knowledge that I talked to said that you should aim to give away about 15% to 20% of the income that's just sitting there. Even though zakat is only 2.5% of your wealth.. You should aim to give up to 20%; which is a very high amount for many of us! Mr. Rizvee was giving me an anecdote on how to save. He was driving a 2000 Toyota Corolla, until recently when he switched to a Mercedes. In 2009, he was the best estate agent in the whole of Canada, yet he was driving a Toyota Corolla! People thought it was a joke. He was still very presentable. But really, he felt it was not about the car. People want value.

Think about it this way. If you're selling a family's house, often their most valuable asset, then you must know what you're doing. Otherwise you could really ruin their financial condition if you're not trained properly. So his main perspective was to know what he was doing, not spending the money. And now he can spend all he wants given the success that ensued.

It's also important not to be extremely stingy, because that doesn't bring wealth either. Being extremely spendthrift or extremely stingy- neither are advisable. If Allah gives you wealth, you have to show it as an example and inspiration to people. It isn't recommended to live in a rundown house if you're a millionaire. You should live according to your means.

'And as for the favor of your Lord, proclaim it!'

- Al-Quran, Surah Ad-Duha, Ayah 11

I was recently in a discussion about just that. One of West Africa's famous Muslim entrepreneurs was noted for his great generosity. He also used a private jet frequently to go to Makkah and attend Umrah or Jummah. He is after all the richest man in all of Africa, worth close to $20 billion.

Is that wasteful for a successful Muslim Entrepreneur? Not at all. A private jet might represent 1/1000th of his net worth, yet, many ordinary people are known to spend over 1/10th of their net worth on a new car. Who is saving more? In this case, it is the billionaire with his private jet!

GIVING IS INVESTING

The most successful Muslim entrepreneurs are also the biggest givers. You should aim at becoming a millionaire entrepreneur not because of the things you can buy, all the mansions you can live in, all the cars you can drive …

Now, those things are great! They are fun! But you should aim at becoming a millionaire Muslim Entrepreneur because of what you give.

Don't let anybody make you feel guilty about setting a goal to become wealthy. If someone does, I challenge them to give as much as you will give once you are wealthy.

How much should you give? I repeat Imam Ashraf's suggestion that is based on the Sunnah of the prophet SAW. Give 10% and your business will not go down. Give 33% and your business will have no choice but to strive.

This is of your net profit; what you bring home. Now, 33% seems like a lot but we know that in many Western countries, Muslims are paying the government that much in taxes. If not more! So it is very reasonable. It all depends on how much you want to make.

MANAGING THE MONEY

It sounds like a job for some kind of fund manager of a Fortune 500 company!

No, you don't have to be that big to manage money. You just need, let's say $100 to get started. Get started with what you have. I remember learning to save money with pennies back in Senegal. If you do it long enough, you end up becoming pretty rich. I got to the point where I used to lend money to other people. Just from saving a few pennies every day, you become pretty wealthy.

Managing your money is a mindset. It's not about how much you earn. It's how much you keep. So I want you to shift your mindset from "big spending" to "big savings". Ask yourself; how much am I keeping?

Managing your money is also about how much you invest into your venture. I interviewed a lot of people and most of them didn't advise to go into debt just to finance the business. So it's something to be careful about especially nowadays with banks and usury. That's because it's very stressful for people when they get into debt. Some people can make it. Many don't. I wouldn't advise it after following the advice of the successful Muslim Entrepreneurs I interviewed. Most of them did it on their own, at least in the beginning, and then raised funds later.

DEATH OR TAXES

Islamically, tax is something that is frowned upon. The majority of the scholars say it isn't Islamic. Yet, you have to keep in mind that depending on where you live, you must abide to the law of the country.
That, of course, is the smartest thing to do.

In my first year of business, I got a $7,000 refund on my taxes. That was because my business didn't make much money! The venture was not profitable. But it goes to show that it's a good idea to be honest with the tax system. In North America, refunds are in place in case you lose money. But the goal is once you start getting into hundreds of thousands and eventually millions, you will be comfortable giving an ample amount of tax.

The good news is income you earn through business ventures is less taxed than the income you earn through being an employee.

Being an employee can become very expensive for you because you will pay so much tax. Say, you pay up to 40% of your six figure salary in taxes annually. Annually! That's huge! Every year you lose money. And it compounds. That is why tax is your biggest expense.

Despite this, according to the expert accountant Salim Siddiqi, you should never take a business decision and make it a tax decision. Your decision should always be just for business reasons.

The reason being is you sometimes need to spend a dollar to save twenty cents in tax. So it doesn't make sense to spend money to make a tax cut. You should just make business decisions. The reality remains that tax is here. Sure, we hope it disappears so we can get richer.

Fortunately, some of the Muslim majority countries like Saudi Arabia, Qatar and Oman do not charge any tax. You can get richer there, maybe. It's something worth thinking about.

2

THE DIFFERENT INDUSTRIES

REAL-ESTATE EMPIRES

Real estate is something here to stay. People need a place to live all the time.

From the Hadith reported by Imam Ahmad, we learn the prophet SAW gave advice about real estate:

> "Whoever sells a house or piece of land then does not put its price into something similar, will not be blessed therein."

When people were selling houses in Madinah, the prophet SAW advised to reinvest that money into more houses. Thus, 1,400 years ago, Muslims knew about supply and demand.

Real estate is a very old industry. How can you use it? Well, you need to know that field before you invest in it. There is a lot of speculation in it. A lot of people got burnt because of pitfalls like usury and speculation.

Without those things, real estate is a blessed field. I think again about Azim Rizvee and his knowledge of the terrain he sells.
He knew everything, up to the type of the soil! That way, he can recognise the right kind of investment. From family experience, reading and being interested in the field, he was able to master real estate. At one point, every second day, he was selling a house. Which is very remarkable. It's more houses sold by a single person than an entire agency; those agents had no business training. Mr. Rizvee found it ridiculous that people would go into real estate with no funding, no training, no research.

So if you want to get into this field, know your art. Contact people that know what they're doing in the area you want to go into. It's a risky venture; a lot of people lose money. But those who know what they're doing win big time.

Salim Siddiqi built a million dollar house for himself because you don't pay tax on a principle place of residence. But it's not just about escaping tax. It's about real estate being a very wise investment; if you know what you're doing.

NETWORK MARKETING

There is no right or wrong business. Look around you. You'll see very successful people in every field. You'll also see unsuccessful people in every field (they are the majority). So it isn't the field itself. It's the mindset of the person working.

That is why I spend so much time talking about the mindset of the Muslim Entrepreneur. Find out what the Muslim Entrepreneur thinks about wealth before joining the ranks of the entrepreneurs.

But you see, it shouldn't just stop there. A lot of you want success. You're hungry for it. A lot of you work on your mental attitude. You believe in yourself. You read a lot of stories of people who made it before you. And you know you can do it. But you shouldn't stop there. To really change the way we think sometimes, we need other people to show us the way.

One of the best ways I have found is network marketing. It is a system of selling and distributing products and services through other people. Like building companies within companies. You get a cut of a commission depending on the sale volume you generate. It's a nice concept, with its own ups and downs. But what I can tell you is it's an easy first step into business. Some companies only charge $50 to at most $1,000 to start your own business. From personal experience, having started a restaurant business myself, I can tell you that an average enterprise will cost you way more than those amounts.

Therefore, it is an easy way to get your feet wet. You could even become a millionaire. A lot of them do. A lot fail too. Some people become rich; a lot of them don't make it. But you get the business education you need to succeed. It's not necessary to go that route, but it can help you improve your communication skills through personal development. Most companies provide growth and leadership seminars on top of some reading material. It's a nice way to develop skills in the race to success. It's challenging and competitive. Go for it if you can get a plus by getting more educated.

But, like in any other business, I would really advise to screen what you're getting into before you join a Network Marketing organization. Check the product out; decide if it's worth it for you. Once you're satisfied; go for it! Look for someone that can really teach and mentor you in the business. You will benefit tremendously.

For Muslim Entrepreneurs, I think it's a good concept, because if you share something good Allah rewards you as well as the person who did the good. That exists in network marketing too. If you introduce someone to the product, and he builds a sales organization, you too will prosper.

PROTOTYPE

Manufacturing is still the order of the day for entrepreneurs in Africa, East Asia, Europe, etc. A lot of people are still involved in making things. That is manufacturing; making physical things you can sell.

I'm thinking of the hobby-craft entrepreneur Dr. Zahoor Qureshi who does hand printing, greeting and wedding cards.

He distributes his material all over the world. Manufacturing is still here. It's just shifted.
It's not just about the volume but the quality of the product.

It generally requires more investment than other ventures, but you can start with a prototype. When you invent something good, build the prototype. I'm thinking of Dr. Hatim Zaghloul. He and his colleague were the main inventors of Wifi technology. He started the company in the 1990s. It was at the top of the world. To this day, companies like Apple and Motorola are using their patent to do business. By the early 2000s, it was truly one of the most important companies in terms of wireless technology. Now the first thing he had to do to secure funds and grow the business was to build a prototype. It took off shortly after.

So manufacturing is still relevant. You just need to know what you're doing. Build the prototype first. Test it and market it. That way you can avoid putting in money that you don't have.

TODAY'S GOLD-RUSH

The internet is huge. The internet is making business a whole lot easier and faster. With this exchange of information, you can have any kind of knowledge. Even religious knowledge.

Even though things like manners and akhlaq can't be learnt from YouTube, you can still do a fair amount of research. The internet is still very powerful.

Now, how does this apply to your business? Prior to the Internet, salesmen used to have to physically go to a client, knock at their door and do business. There was no other way. Nowadays, you can just sit at home, build your own business, and have people process a transaction virtually. You make your commission that way. There are many models out there. What I can tell you for sure is the internet has made it a lot faster to distribute goods all over the world.

How can you benefit? You don't need to be an expert, but learn enough to hire people to do the hard bits for you. Today, you can hire people that can build your websites for you or program for your venture. It's pretty easy.

The final benefit of the internet is that it really has the potential to do business from anywhere in the world. For many years, people had to move to high income locations to work for forty years and have a good lifestyle. Nowadays, with the internet, I've met several entrepreneurs that are living the 'dream' lifestyle from all over the world. They could be living in the Middle East, yet, are making millions per year whilst sleeping and spending time with family! Obviously they work hard, but the internet has made it easy to be on the beach and earn money. Your store is constantly online, open at all hours for people to make a purchase.

But remember, you need to look for a reliable mentor. I offer live mentoring services over the internet, to teach people how to really build their business. So I recommend you do the research and find the right person to work with.

Remember: the internet is a levelling ground. You could be in Africa, living modestly, yet, become very wealthy through the internet.

If you have an internet connection, you can become rich. A lot of people are getting into it. It's becoming more and more competitive. But the goldmine that is the internet is still a good way to get into entrepreneurship.

Muhammad Fattal, a 22 years old entrepreneur started his tech company with no capital. Born in Syria, he moved to Saudi Arabia then to Canada. He saw the gap between Social Media use in the Middle East and North America. His dad knew an artist in Saudi Arabia and Muhammad just decided to call him and offered his services. He would help him to have a presence on social media. The artist said yes. That was his first client! Today, after only 3 years, he has well over one billion views on the channels his company manages.

'Don't be afraid to pickup the phone!'

- Muhammad Fattal, Founder of the Alfan Group

BANKING

Some people prefer to go through the route of the banking system to finance their ventures. Now, that has its own pros and cons.

The majority of the scholars say it is not allowed because of the element of interest. This discussion is however beyond the scope of this book.

The bottom line is that you need to know what you are doing. The primary reason banking should exist at all is to finance businesses that don't have the funds but are expecting to yield a return.

Islamic banking could be an option but is more limited. I believe banking helps the economy tremendously. It's always more expensive to raise stock than to outright borrow money. So what a lot of companies do is they balance offering stock for the initial investment whilst doing a public offering.

You can also raise funds and make your own bank and offer stock to the public at a later stage. Remember, banking can be very profitable as a business venture as well.

VENTURE CAPITAL

The foremost expert I found was Dr. Hatim Zaghloul, who, in a span of ten years started over six companies that went public.
He is a very accomplished businessman. Now, he is building technological companies in Egypt. Always in the building mode. That's someone you may want to consult about the stock and financial market. He knows the game. He knows how to do things properly.

Dr. Hatim Zaghloul told me you only need a capitalization of $500,000 in assets that are sitting there in the company in order to make it go public. It's not something unfeasible. I know a lot of people get scared about such a move. But if you have the right structure and the right business experience, it's possible.

Now, why don't more people go into the financial market?

Why isn't it more widespread than banking? Why is banking more popular? Well a lot of it is due to ignorance. Islam really encourages financial markets. Raising funds to go into business is encouraged. Partnerships are after all made by pooling resources and sharing the returns. The stock market is just an elongated, more sophisticated version of that process. A whole lot of people that don't necessarily know each other personally buy into a company and share the profits and losses. It's a very Islamic idea.

Dr. Hatim raised hundreds of millions of dollars from investors when he was building his technology ventures Wi Lan and Cell-Loc.

So you may want to look into financial markets. If you have a technology company for example and need extra funding, the idea is viable.

AN ENDLESS HARVEST

.

Muslims have always produced many books. At the peak of its success, books were more expensive to buy than gold in the Empire of Mali. In Syria, scholars like Ibn Qayyim wrote hundreds of books during their lifetime. They could write two hundred, four hundred books, yet it would not be something out of the ordinary.

Nowadays, art and publishing are still very much alive. Yet you don't hear it a whole lot in the mainstream media. But there are people producing high quality work.

I'm thinking about the Khayyal theatre in London. Like them, a lot of Muslims are producing very high quality work.

There are people publishing works of art and works of philosophy, fiction, video games... all kinds of things nowadays.

In the area of professional photography, I had the opportunity to interview Peter Sanders. He produces books on photography and earns commissions through governments or directly with people. And this is really residual income.

Every time someone uses the photograph, the artist gets paid.

However, for the uninitiated into the ways of residual income, publishing and the arts aren't very exciting. It's more exciting to become a doctor, a lawyer or an engineer. Yes, as an artist or a writer, you'll notice there may be some years of financial difficulty. Yes, it might be tough in the beginning. Yes, people may not cheer for you at the very start. But if you put in that effort it will eventually yield residual income.

3

YOUR PATH TO WEALTH

FROM EMPLOYEE TO ENTREPRENEUR

You go to school, graduate and somehow you've got to start doing something. Some people start directly. They become entrepreneurs because they know what they want.

Say you've been writing computer code since you were in school. By the time you're 23 and out of college, you could start a company, really. That's something I encourage. Get your children interested in a hobby they love, that can become a skill. Be interested in raising empowered children.

Now, the most popular thing to do once people leave school is to become an employee.

But we've just seen from considering how much tax one has to pay, that an employee is in the highest tax bracket. They have to pay the most tax. And they have no control over their time.

So what some people will do is start a business. That is the purpose of this book. To become a Muslim Entrepreneur. That is the most viable way to become financially strong and free.

In North America alone, through a survey done by the Federal Reserve, people that are running businesses have five times the net worth of people that are employed. Five times! That gives you a perspective.

What you can do after becoming an entrepreneur is make sure you automate the business. Make sure to look for a mentor that can show you the way if you don't know how to do that. Once you get the business going and it's growing, gradually make your income residual. Aim to own assets like rentals or a parking space, where people will pay you over and over again. Or patent something. Or write a book. Or create something artistic. And just collect the fees!

I'm thinking of Mrs. Lena Khan who is finishing up her next film. She's in California right now raising money for her venture. A very excited sister with tremendous talent. And she saves every penny. Even our interview was done over her home phone number to avoid the cost of a cell call! That's how focused she is as an entrepreneur about building her dream and her business.

She is working for residual income. Once the movie is out, as a director she will collect the fees. She will get the money for every theatre that plays her film.

It's very exciting to have residual income. Think about ways you can get it done. You can also invest in other ventures so you can share in the process. Both ways, you become very wealthy.

THE GOLDEN TOUCH

Have you noticed that some people just seem to have that touch? They just seem to know where the money is and make a profit very quickly, whilst others struggle along. Firstly, one of their traits is that they are open to opportunity.

Azim Rizvee says, "do not put a price tag on yourself. At the end of the day, you have to be open to all the possibilities in order to turn those possibilities into profit."

Secondly, know that you cannot just decide to go into business. Say you decide to run a cosmetics business and you don't know the first thing about working in a salon. In that case, it would be very difficult for you to make a profit! A smarter way would be to know the business inside out.

As a young man, Azim Rizvee learnt the brokerage business from his family; his father and grandfather were entrepreneurs themselves and taught him about real estate. So he was very young when he became familiar with his trade.

He picked up details like how to know the soil the property is built on. That's pretty useful here in Canada, given how much people love their gardens! Details like that made him an expert on selling houses.

He would study each property even further; he would give details of the area, what the drainage was like, if the land could flood and so on. What homeowners would want to know before spending half a million dollars on a property.

That is how you can really boost your business to the next level. Know the industry inside out. All of the best are experts in their area; Dr. Amina Coxon for example was trained at John Hopkins in New York, the best hospital in the USA. With that kind of training, it's no wonder she was able to open a physician's practice on Harley Street in London, one of the most exclusive areas to practice as a doctor in that country. She has the training.

Dr. Amina learns very efficiently, like in the case I mentioned where she diagnosed a patient with a disease she hadn't seen in 20 years in just under 15 minutes. This is because she has mastered her profession, as well as how to learn about it. She knows the subject inside out and doesn't have to waste time recalling things. So her patients are amazed! They are so impressed with her efficiency and honesty, especially because her practice is private. If she chose to take longer, she could make more money, but she knows that isn't the best way to ensure good quality customer service. Thanks to her speed, Dr. Amina has more time for her family, more time for her private studies and so on. So the benefit of learning your trade is many fold.

REINVEST IN YOURSELF

Now that you have the business going, invest in yourself, first and foremost.

Learn the skills. Develop your communication skills. Learn the right business skills. And this learning is constant. It never stops. Technology and development in your field is not stopping after all, so why would you stop?

One of the things I learnt from Nazir Ahmed is when he told me is that a lot of people start their business but they remain small all their lives, meaning they don't grow beyond a certain point. Ususally, it is because their skills are not developed enough.

You have to keep growing to keep up with the times, so to speak. So if technical skills are lacking, learn them. If contacts are lacking, get them. Do whatever is necessary to grow. Since technology is constantly advancing, people whose products and services are out-dated they struggle in the marketplace. What you want to do is to become a leader in your field.

Mr. Rizvee became one because he was innovative. He set up the business in such a way that out-produced all of the competition for years to come. That was because of his system. A lot of the competition now is copying his marketing strategy. That doesn't bother him however, because as a business leader you have to share.

What you want to do is become the leader and then create a movement that is positive for your customer, for your community and for the general good.

Reinvest a percentage of revenue in the business that will go back into your business so that you don't eat your capital. Invest back your money, then, budget what you will save as well as what you will give. After that, budget your personal spending.

THE GENE OF SUCCESS

Some Muslim entrepreneurs started broke. Like the family of Salim Siddiqi, who went through partition and war. Many people died in those years and it was very sad. But they persevered and became successful. You see, it's something I call the gene of success. Nobody is condemned to failure or success, but when you see your entire family become successful, it's not just by chance. There are deeper explanations to those things. It comes from belief that it can be done, because it has been done in the past already.

Let's say my baby wants to walk. Our baby will see his parents walking, he sees everyone around him walking, talking and jumping around. Soon enough he too will imitate what people around him do.

Why is that? It is a part of the gene of success. You've been successful in walking. It wasn't easy. You probably stumbled a few times in the beginning, hurt yourself ... but you walked! And now you can do all kinds of things whilst walking, almost on auto pilot. So the baby observes all of that and thinks to himself, "obviously I have to walk too, because I'm a human, and I see all these humans walking!" And that's how you want to see success as well.

See yourself as a baby that is learning something for the first time. If you fall, no big deal. You fall, you giggle, or you cry- in the end, you get back up. The baby doesn't take it personally. He thinks "everybody is doing it, I can do it too!" That's the attitude of a winner. That is the gene of success.

You look around you and you say: "look at all these Muslim Entrepreneurs that have been successful, I can succeed as well!" That is why, when people that are born into a business family or a family of lawyers or doctors, they are likely to become that too. Because there is a success gene where they've seen someone else do it before. It becomes easier.

So what I want you to do is identify people that believe the same things you believe. And observe them. See that they are normal people, with normal lives and normal families. They may sometimes be less scholarly or educated than you. But if they have been successful, it means you too can be successful. And that is the key ingredient to success. You look at other people. Then you look at yourself and say, "you know what? If they did it, I can do it."

I'll just end with the example of Yaya Ndianor, a successful Senegalese entrepreneur. He started broke. He travelled with his brothers to Central Africa and the Congo, where they settled down. That was until a conflict erupted. They were imprisoned, with people pointing guns at them. They barely escaped with their lives.

That disaster gave him the strength to say, "you know what, I've almost died going after my goals and dreams. But I'm still here. That means I can do this!" Now he is a wealthy.

There are many stories like that. But all I can tell you is if you have a house, a bed, a job, or you're studying … you're ahead of so many people.

When we count the blessings of Allah, there are so many of them. We cannot possibly enumerate them all. So see yourself as successful.
When you look in the mirror, say "well, if all of these people are doing it, so can I!"

NOW, GET A MENTOR

Seek a mentor right now! Don't wait.

Why do you want a mentor? Because they will influence you.

The first thing to understand is that you on average are worth within $2000 of your closest friend. Now I'm not saying that as a Muslim, you should only hang out with people that are wealthy. That isn't our mentality at all. Rather, arrange your friendship circles in groups. When you need advice on business, go to business minded people. When you need company for your deen, spend your time with people that fear Allah SWT and have deen. Now when I say deen it also envelopes good akhlaq, good character, good disposition.

Avoid your broke friends when seeking business advice!

If you don't know any millionaires, reach out to me. I can teach you how to build connections with people that have the results you want.

Let's say I want to travel from Ontario to Morocco by boat. Say I go to the East Coast of Canada in the summer. I set off. I just go east. I could hit England, France, or Greenland. Where should I go? It's anyone's guess. But what if I had a professional navigator with me? Or a GPS that has already gotten someone through the same journey? How much easier would that be?

Now think about someone who has already done what you are trying to do. Someone like you; a Muslim Entrepreneur that has accomplished your desire goal. Seek out their mentorship. Don't waste any time. I highly recommend it.

A mentor will also keep you accountable. Don't pick someone that will sugar coat for you. I learnt tremendously from the mentors I interviewed. Because they will tell you the truth and the truth hurts sometimes. But you have to keep in mind that the truth can set you free.

FINAL WORDS

Being an entrepreneur doesn't guarantee you happiness. But it can set you free. With freedom of choice and freedom to do what you enjoy doing, whether for this world or the hereafter.

So many Muslims dream of doing great things. However, they don't have the funds, and their jobs keep their time locked.

It's a shame. I have seen far too many very well intentioned Muslims that are unable to live out their dreams to the fullest because they're just too busy working for someone else's dream. Just so they can pay the bills and survive.

They work for forty years, yet remain financially insecure.

My only advice to you is this: change your plan. Become a Muslim Entrepreneur. You need this. Your family needs it. The Ummah needs it.

It has been an honour to write this book for you, and I hope I can continue to serve you further.

For your success,
Assalamu Aleykum

Oumar Soule

THE AUTHOR

Oumar Soule is a scholar of Financial Mathematics engaged in the study of stock markets. He holds a PhD in Mathematics of Finance from McMaster University, Canada.

By helping Muslim entrepreneurs identify opportunities and connect with each other, he has become a much sought after business consultant.

The much anticipated seminar series accompanying this book is designed to help up-and-coming Muslim Entrepeneurs to jump-start their business.

THE MUSLIM ENTREPRENEUR

www.the-muslim-entrepreneur.com
oumar@the-muslim-entrepreneur.com

Printed in the USA
CPSIA information can be obtained
at www.ICGtesting.com
LVHW090235311223
767624LV00059B/1103